CLIL/Culture	Values	Phonics	I can...
Math: School possessions notebook, pencil case, pencil sharpener, tablet How many pencils do you have? I have three pencils. **Around the World: Classrooms**	Be polite. Thank you. You're welcome. Please sit down.	a, t, p, n an, ant, at tan, tap pan, pant, pat nap	...name classroom objects. ...talk about the things I have and about rules. ...be polite.
Social Science: Gender baby, best friend, boy, girl, love, man, woman This woman is my mom. This girl is my sister. This is my sister. **Around the World: Families**	Help your family. Can I help you? Yes, thank you. Please help me. OK. I can help you.	i, s, b, d in, is, it, pin sad, sit bad, bat dad, dip	...talk about my family. ...say how many brothers and sisters I have. ...ask to help my family.
Science: The senses cake, flower, guitar, hear, ice cream, picture, see, smell, taste, teddy bear, TV I see/taste/hear/smell with my ... **Around the World: Flags**	Keep clean. Wash with soap. Rinse with water. Dry your hands.	e, c, g, m pen, pet cap, cat gas, get, wig map, mat	...name one or more parts of the body. ...talk about my senses. ...say how I keep clean.
Social Science: Weather and clothing cold, desert, dry, hot, jungle, mountains, wet It's cold in the mountains. I'm wearing a jacket. **Around the World: Funny hats**	Respect all cultures. They're wearing traditional clothes from Guatemala.	o, k, ck dog, on, pot kid, kite kick, neck, pick, sock	...say what people are wearing and their age. ...talk about clothes. ...respect all cultures.
Art: Shapes apartment, circle, houseboat, lighthouse, rectangle, square, yurt **Around the World: Homes** bathroom, bedroom, comfortable, dining room, kitchen, living room, motor home, trailer park	Help at home. He's washing the dishes. She's drying the dishes. She's cleaning her room. She's helping her parents.	u, f, ff run, sun, up fan, fog, fun off, puff	...talk about home activities. ...name shapes in homes and describe things. ...talk about helping at home.
Social Science: Baby animals calf, chick, kitten, puppy A baby chicken is called a chick. **Around the World: Pets** canary, hamster, mouse, pet, snake	Be nice to animals. feeding, walking I'm feeding the chicks.	r, h, j red, rock, run hat, hen, hut jam, jet, job	...talk about what animals and baby animals are doing. ...talk about possessions. ...say how to be nice to animals.
Science: Sweet and salty food chips, chocolate, cookies, fries, salt, salty, sugar, sweet Chips are salty. Chocolate is sweet. **Around the World: Special food** birthday, candy, pie, (seaweed) soup	Eat three meals a day. I eat breakfast every day. I eat lunch every day. I eat dinner every day. I eat salad for lunch every day.	l, ll, v, w leg, let bell, doll, tall van, vet we, web, win	...talk about party food. ...ask and answer about what people have. ...name sweet and salty food.
Art: Kites bird, butterfly, dragon, fish This kite looks like a fish. It's green. **Around the World: Favorite toys**	Share your toys. Sharing is fun! Here's my car. Let's share. Okay. Thank you!	qu, x, y quack, quick box, fox, ox, six yell, yes, yum	...name toys. ...say where something is. ...talk about sharing my toys.
Physical Education: Playground games climb, hide and seek, hop, hopscotch, tag Let's play hide and seek. **Around the World: The same game** paper, player, rock, scissors, win	Take care of your body. Get enough exercise. Get enough sleep. Get enough food and drink.	ss, z, zz kiss, mess, miss zap, zip buzz, fizz, jazz	...talk about actions and what I like/don't like. ...talk about games children play. ...say how I take care of my body.

3

Welcome to Class!

1 🎧 **Listen, look, and say.**

BIG ENGLISH 1 PLUS

Mario Herrera • Christopher Sol Cruz

STUDENT'S BOOK

Contents

Unit	Vocabulary	Structures
Welcome to Class! pp. 4–9	student, teacher, window **Classroom language:** clap your hands, close your book, open your book, pick up your pencil, point to the door, raise your hand, sit down, stand up, turn around **Shapes:** circle, heart, rectangle, square, star, triangle **Colors:** black, blue, brown, green, gray, orange, pink, purple, red, white, yellow **Numbers:** 1–15	Hello! What's your name? I'm... Goodbye! How are you? I'm fine, thanks. What is it? It's a triangle. Is it a square? No./Yes. What color is it? It's blue. It's a blue circle. What's your favorite color? My favorite color is... How many...? How old are you? I'm...
1 Good Morning, Class! pp. 10–25	**Classroom items:** backpack, book, chair, crayon, desk, eraser, marker, pen, pencil, ruler	What is it? It's a pen. What are they? They're green pens. Stand up! Raise your hand! Don't talk!
2 My Family pp. 26–41	**Family members:** brother, dad, grandpa, grandma, grandparents, mom, parents, sister **Other:** photo album	Who's he? He's my brother. Who are they? They're my sisters. How many brothers do you have? I have two brothers. This is my dad. These are my parents. Her name's Megan.
3 My Body pp. 42–57	**Parts of the body:** arm, ear, eye, finger, foot/feet, hand, head, leg, mouth, neck, nose, toe **Size:** big, long, short, small **Other:** hair	Do you have big eyes? Yes, I do. Does she have long hair? Yes, she does. Does he have short hair? No, he doesn't. He has long hair. It's a desk. It's an eraser. They're crayons.
Checkpoint Units 1–3 pp. 58–61	**Units 1–3 Exam Preparation** pp. 62–63	
4 My Favorite Clothes pp. 64–79	**Clothing items:** blouse, boots, dress, gloves, hat, jacket, pants, shirt, shoes, shorts, skirt, socks, T-shirt	What are you wearing? I'm wearing a green hat. What's she wearing? She's wearing red pants. How old are you? I'm seven. How old is she? She's nine. How old are they? They're ten.
5 Busy at Home pp. 80–95	**Home activities:** brushing my teeth, combing my hair, drinking, eating, getting dressed, making lunch, playing, reading, sleeping, taking a bath, talking on the phone, washing	What are you doing? I'm talking on the phone. What's he doing? He's eating. What color is it? It's green. What color are they? They're red.
6 On the Farm pp. 96–111	**Animals:** cat, chicken, cow, dog, duck, frog, goat, horse, sheep, turtle **Actions:** eating, flying, jumping, running	What's the goat doing? It's eating. What are the chickens doing? They're running. This is my mom. Her name's Emma.
Checkpoint Units 4–6 pp. 112–115	**Units 4–6 Exam Preparation** pp. 116–117	
7 Party Time pp. 118–133	**Food:** cake, chicken, fries, fruit, ice cream, juice, milk, pasta, pizza, salad, water **Days of the week**	What do you have? I have salad. What does she have? She has milk. We don't eat cake. She doesn't sleep in a chair.
8 Fun and Games pp. 134–149	**Toys:** action figure, ball, bike, blocks, cars, doll, game, plane, puppet, stuffed animal, train **Furniture:** couch, shelf, table, toy box	Where's the ball? It's in the toy box on the shelf. Where are the blocks? They're under the desk. Is there a cake? Yes, there is. Are there fries? No, there aren't. There are sandwiches.
9 Play Time pp. 150–165	**Action words:** catching, dancing, hitting, jumping rope, kicking, riding, singing, skating, throwing	Is she singing? Yes, she is. Are they dancing? No, they aren't. You like horses. You don't like frogs. He likes fruit. He doesn't like salad.
Checkpoint Units 7–9 pp. 166–169	**Units 7–9 Exam Preparation** pp. 170–171	

Young Learners English Practice Starters pp. 172–180
Cutouts pp. 181–185
Big English Song p. 187

2 Listen. Ask and answer.

Hello! What's your name?

I'm Sam. Goodbye!

I'm Anna. What's your name?

Goodbye, Sam!

3 Listen and point.

4 Look at 3 and role-play with your teacher.

5 Read and match.

1 How are you?
2 What's your name?
3 Hello, I'm Mrs. Smith.

a I'm Patrick.
b Hello, Mrs. Smith.
c I'm fine, thanks.

(greetings) Welcome unit

Shapes

5
6 Listen, point, and repeat.

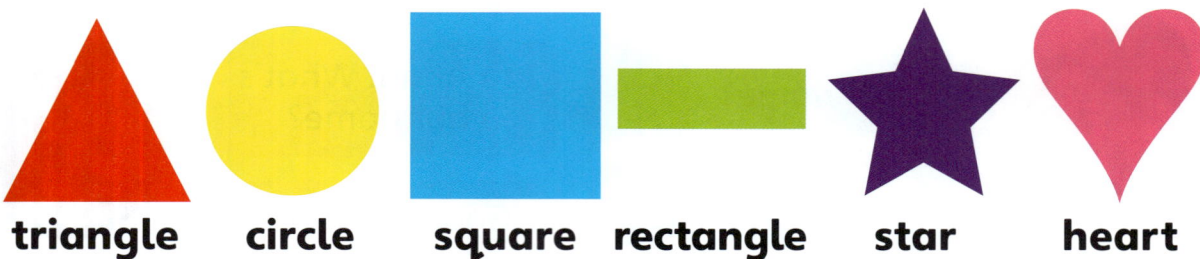

triangle   circle   square   rectangle   star   heart

6
7 Listen and repeat. Then look at 6. Ask and answer.

What is it?   It's a triangle.

7
8 Listen and repeat. Then play a game.

Is it a square?
No.
Is it a heart?
Yes!

6   Welcome unit (shapes)

Colors

9 **Listen, point, and repeat.**

10 **Listen and circle.**

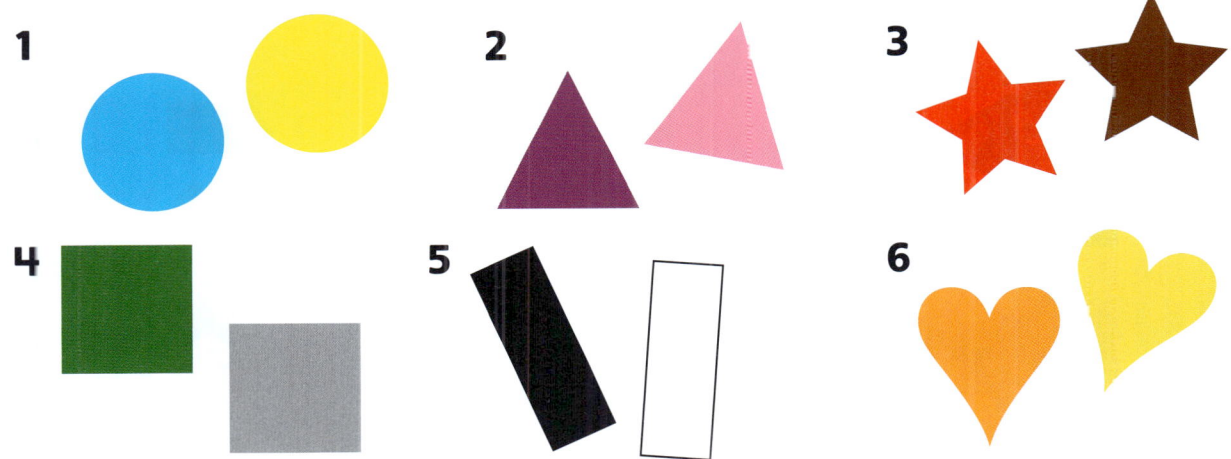

11 **Look at 10. Ask and answer.**

What color is it?

It's blue. It's a blue circle.

12 **Listen and repeat. Then ask the class.**

What's your favorite color?

My favorite color is green.

Name	Favorite color

Numbers

13 **Listen, point, and repeat.**

1 one	2 two	3 three	4 four	5 five
6 six	7 seven	8 eight	9 nine	10 ten
11 eleven	12 twelve	13 thirteen	14 fourteen	15 fifteen

14 **Count the shapes. Then listen and check.**

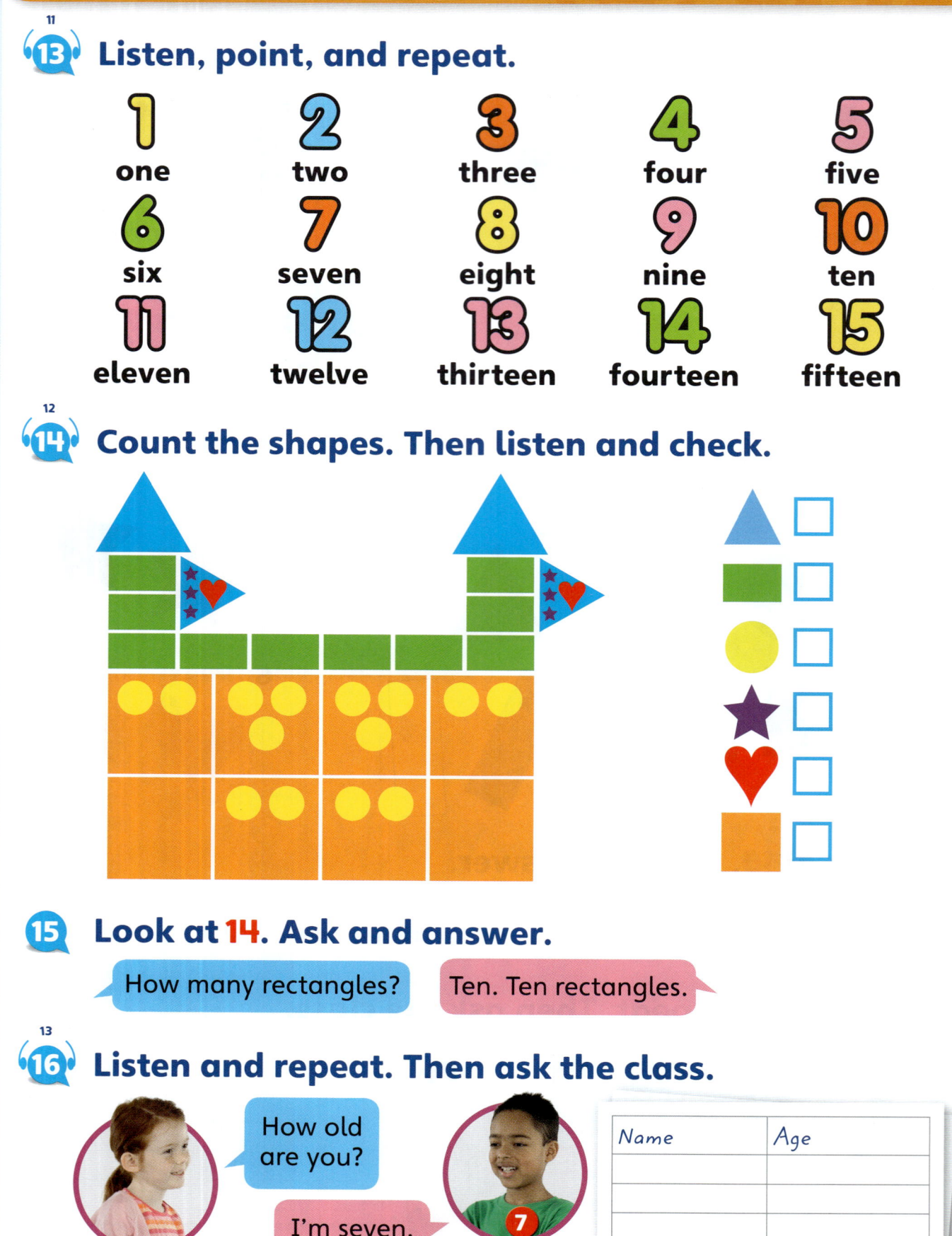

15 **Look at 14. Ask and answer.**

How many rectangles?

Ten. Ten rectangles.

16 **Listen and repeat. Then ask the class.**

How old are you?

I'm seven.

Name	Age

Classroom Language

17 **Listen and chant.**

Listen to the Teacher!

Stand up!
Stand up!
Raise your hand
And turn around!

Point to the window!
Point to the door!
Clap your hands
And sit down!

Pick up your pencil!
Pick up your book!
Open your book
And close your book!

18 **Listen and number.**

a  ☐

b  ☐

c 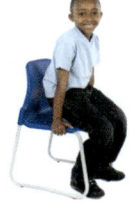 ☐

d  ☐

19 **Play the game.**

Turn around!

Simon says, "Turn around!"

(classroom language) Welcome unit

Good Morning, Class!

1 🎧 **Listen, look, and say.**

1 desk
2 book 
3 crayon 
4 eraser 
5 marker 
6 pen 
7 pencil 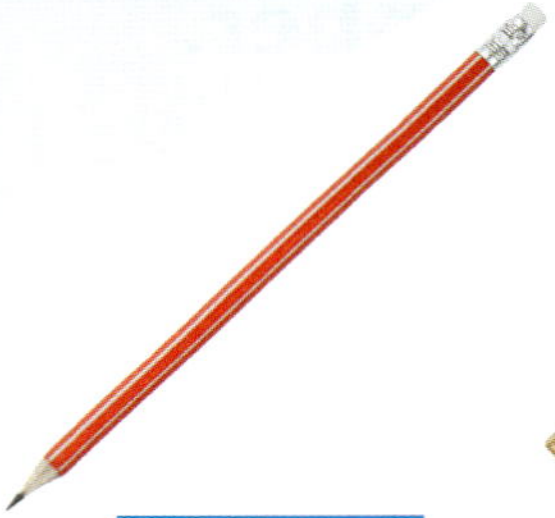
8 ruler 
9 chair 
10 backpack 

2 🎧 **Listen, find, and say.** **3** **Play a game.**

4 Listen and sing. Then look at 1 and find.

The Classroom Song

Good morning, class.
Good morning to you!
How are you?
I'm fine, thank you.

What is it? It's an eraser.
What is it? It's a ruler.
What is it? It's a pencil.
What is it? It's a crayon.

Now pick up your pen
And open your book.
Say the words
And write with me.
Let's start now. 1, 2, 3!

Chorus

5 Listen and number.

a 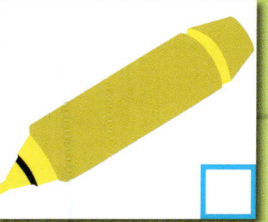 b  c  d

6 Look at 5. Ask and answer.

What is it?

It's a chair.

THINK BIG

What is it? Listen, number, and say.
book ☐   backpack ☐   pencil ☐

song/vocabulary Unit 1 11

Story

7 **Listen and read. What color is the marker?**

"They're red."

"Red? No, Tim. They're green erasers."

"No, look! They're red erasers."

"Tim!"

5

6

8 **Look at the story. Then circle.**

1 a b

2 a b

3 a b

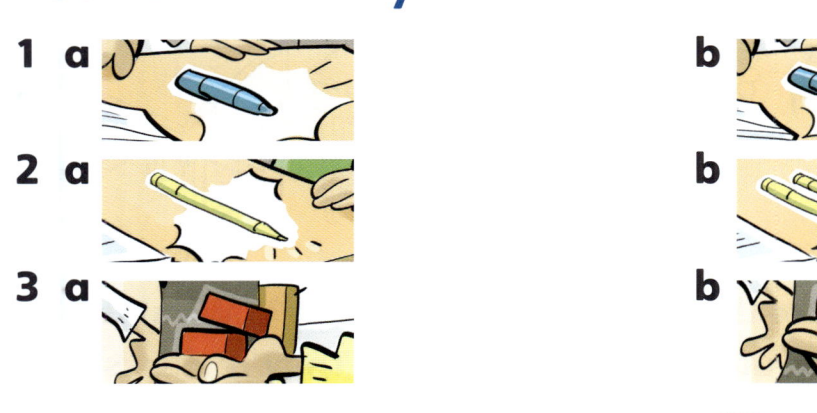

THINK BIG **What happens next? Draw and say.**

Language in Action

9 **Listen. Help Tim and Jane make sentences.**

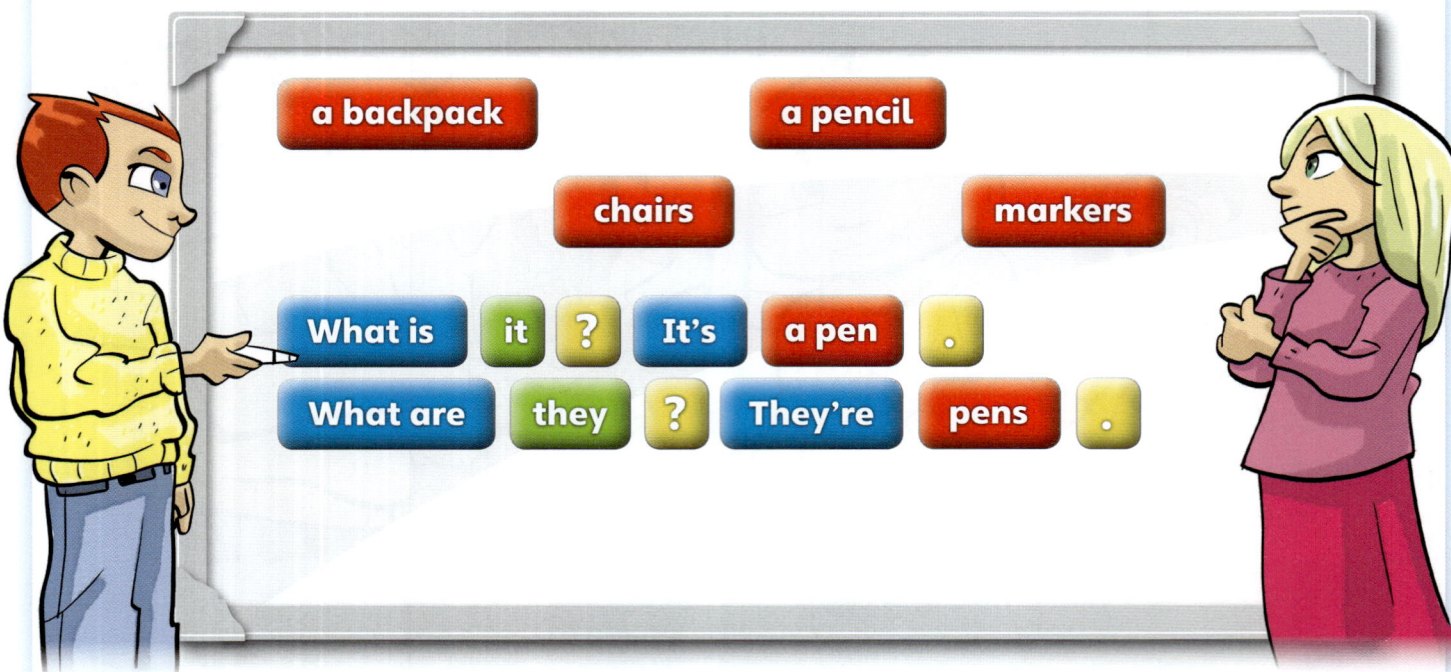

a backpack   a pencil
chairs   markers

What is | it | ? | It's | a pen | .
What are | they | ? | They're | pens | .

10 **Circle and color. Then circle and draw.**

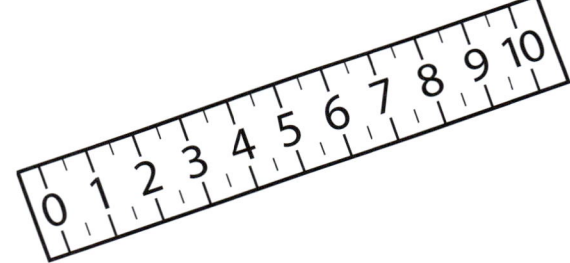

1 What is it? / What are they?
They're rulers. / It's a ruler.
It's blue. / They're blue.

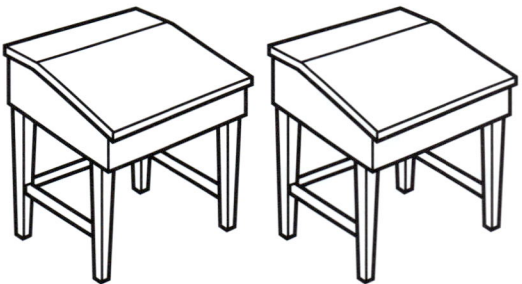

2 What are they? / What is it?
It's a desk. / They're desks.
It's red. / They're red.

3 What is it? / What are they?
They're books. / It's a book.
It's yellow. / They're yellow.

4 What is it? / What are they?
They're erasers. / It's an eraser.
It's brown. / They're brown.

Language in Action

11 **Listen and stick. Then say.**

1 2 3 4

12 **Look at 11. Ask and answer.**

What is it?

What are they?

It's...

They're...

13 **Draw and say.**

language practice (*What are they? They're pencils.*) Unit 1

Content Connection | Math

 14 **Look, listen, and repeat. Then say.**

1 pencil case   2 tablet   3 pencil sharpener   4 notebook

I have a…

 15 **Look, listen, and read. Then match.**

1 Luke — 1 I have a tablet, three notebooks, and a green pencil sharpener.

2 Emma — 2 I have a yellow notebook and a pink pencil sharpener. My pencil case is blue.

3 Ahmed — 3 I have two notebooks and a tablet. My pencil case is purple.

a

b

c

THINK BIG How many…? Say.

16. Look at 15. Count and write.

	pencil sharpener	notebook	pen
Luke			
Emma			
Ahmed			

17. Do a class survey.

	Me		
pencils			
notebooks			
erasers			

How many pencils do you have?

I have seven pencils.

PROJECT

18. Make a My Pencil Case poster. Then present it to the class.

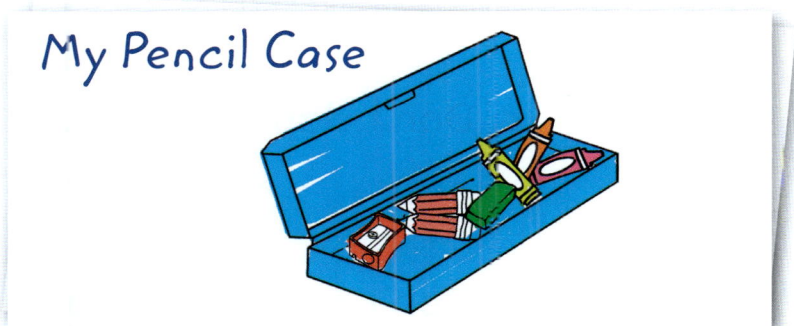

My pencil case is blue. I have…

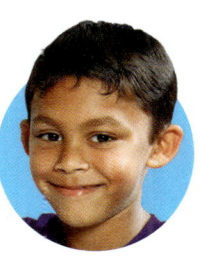

Grammar

19 Look, listen, and repeat.

1  Stand up!

2  Sit down!

3  Look!

4  Don't talk!

5  Don't run!

6  Don't eat!

Stand up!	Don't talk!
Sit down!	Don't run!
Look!	Don't eat!

20 Look, read, and match.

1  a Raise your hand!

2  b Sit down!

3  c Don't clap your hands!

4  d Don't close your book!

Grammar

21 **Read and circle.**

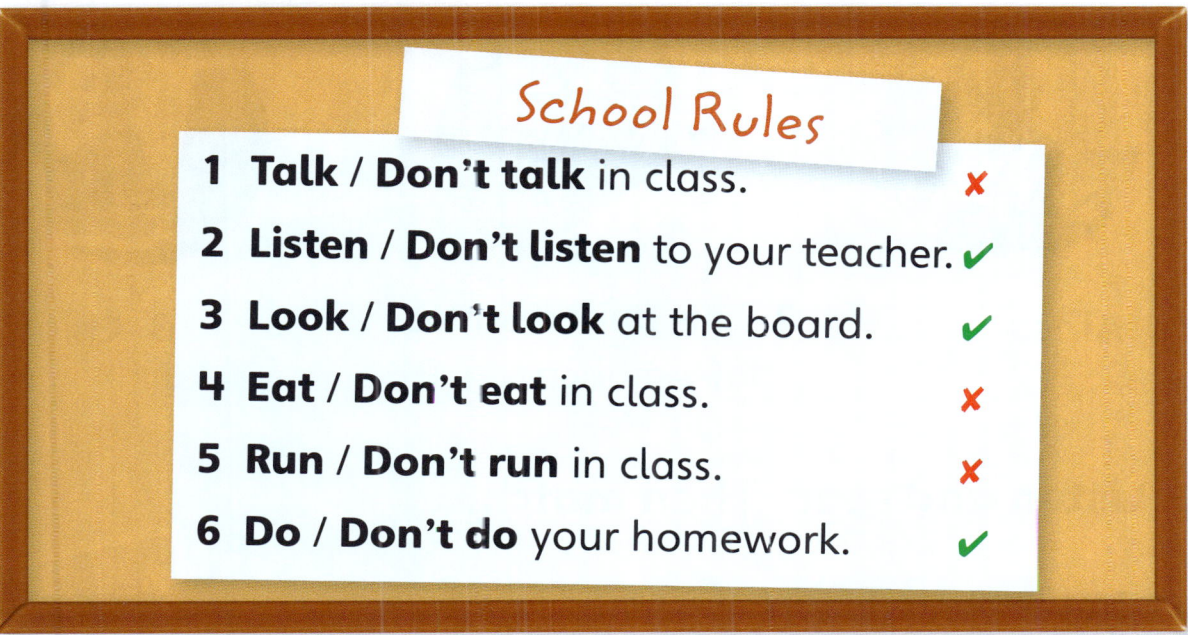

School Rules
1. Talk / **Don't talk** in class. ✗
2. Listen / **Don't listen** to your teacher. ✓
3. **Look** / Don't look at the board. ✓
4. Eat / **Don't eat** in class. ✗
5. Run / **Don't run** in class. ✗
6. **Do** / Don't do your homework. ✓

22 **Play the game.**

Simon says, "Cross your arms!"

Don't cross your arms!

23 **Draw two home rules.**

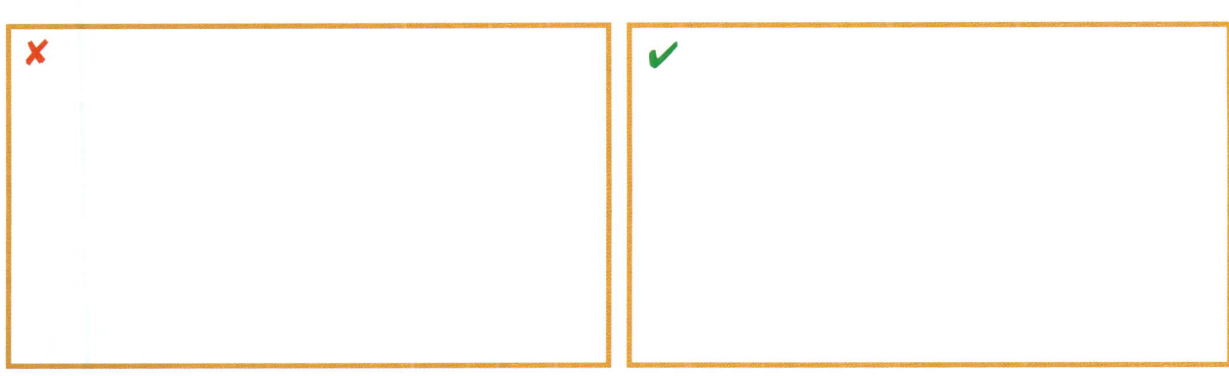

grammar (*Sit down! Don't run!*) Unit 1 **19**

Culture Connection | Around the World

24 Look, listen and repeat.

1 Africa **2** The United States of America **3** China

25 Listen and read. Then match.

1 In the United States of America, I have a big classroom. My desk is small, and my chair is small, too. I have a pencil case, and I have markers, pencils, and crayons. I have an eraser and a ruler, too.

2 My classroom in China is big. My desk is big, too. I have a pen and a notebook. I have a tablet and a green pencil sharpener.

3 This is my classroom in Africa. It's small. I have a small desk. I have a black backpack and a yellow pencil. I have notebooks, too.

a

b

c

26 Look at **25**. Read and ✔.

	Africa	China	USA
black backpack			
tablet			
big desk			
small desk			
big classroom			
notebook			
yellow pencil			

27 What do you have on your desk? Draw and say.

It's a… . They're… .

THINK BIG What can you find in classrooms everywhere?

culture connection (classrooms) Unit 1 **21**

Values | Be polite.

28 **Listen and find the picture. Then listen and repeat.**

29 **Look and number. Then say.**

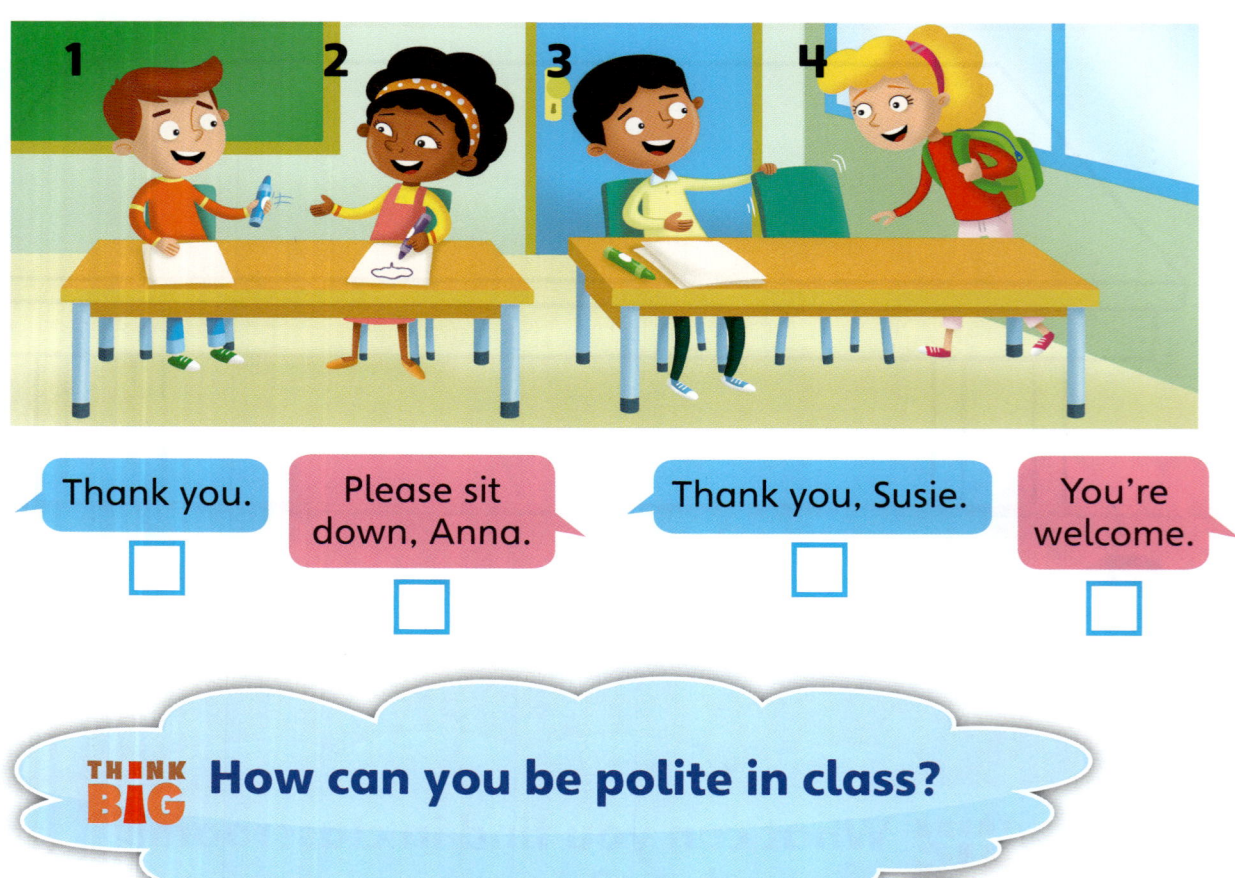

Thank you. ☐ Please sit down, Anna. ☐ Thank you, Susie. ☐ You're welcome. ☐

THINK BIG How can you be polite in class?

a, t, p, n | Phonics

 30 Listen, look, and repeat.

1 a 2 t 3 p 4 n

 31 Listen and find. Then say.

pan   ant   nap   tap

 32 Listen and blend the sounds.

1 a-n   an   2 p-a-t   pat
3 p-a-n-t   pant 4 t-a-n   tan
5 a-t   at

 33 Underline a, t, p, and n. Then listen and chant.

Pat the ant
Has a tan.
Pat the ant
Takes a nap.

phonics (a, t, p, n) Unit 1 **23**

Review

 Look and find the differences. Then listen and check.

Picture A

Picture B

 Listen and play a game.

Review

🎧 36 Listen and circle.

1

2

3

37 Read and match.

1 Don't run!

2 Sit down!

3 Please don't talk!

4 Eat, please!

a

b

c

d

I Can

☐ name classroom objects.
☐ talk about the things I have and about rules.
☐ be polite.

My Family

1 Listen, look, and say.

1 grandpa
2 grandma
3 mom
4 dad
5 brother
6 sister
7 me
8 parents (mom and dad)
9 grandparents (grandma and grandpa)

2 Listen, find, and say.   **3** Play a game.

Unit 2 vocabulary (family members)

4 Listen and sing. Then look at 1 and find.

My Family

My family, my family!
This is my family.
He's my brother
And she's my sister.

My dad, my mom!
My sister, my brother!
We have so much fun!
I love them.

My family, my family.
I love my family!
I love them,
And they love me.
I love my family!

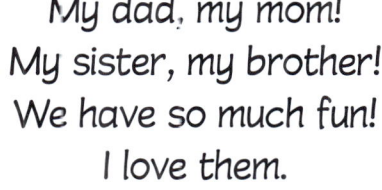

5 Look at 4 and circle the correct answer.

1 grandpa / dad   2 grandma / sister
3 mom / brother   4 sister / brother

6 Look at 4. Ask and answer.

 Who's he?

He's my grandpa.

THINK BIG Are all families the same? Who's in your family?

Story

 7 Listen and read. How many brothers? How many sisters?

8 **Look at the story. Then circle.**

1 She's my mom.

2 He's my dad.

3 They're my brother and sister.

THINK BIG Who's missing? Draw.

Language in Action

9 **Listen. Help Tim and Jane make sentences.**

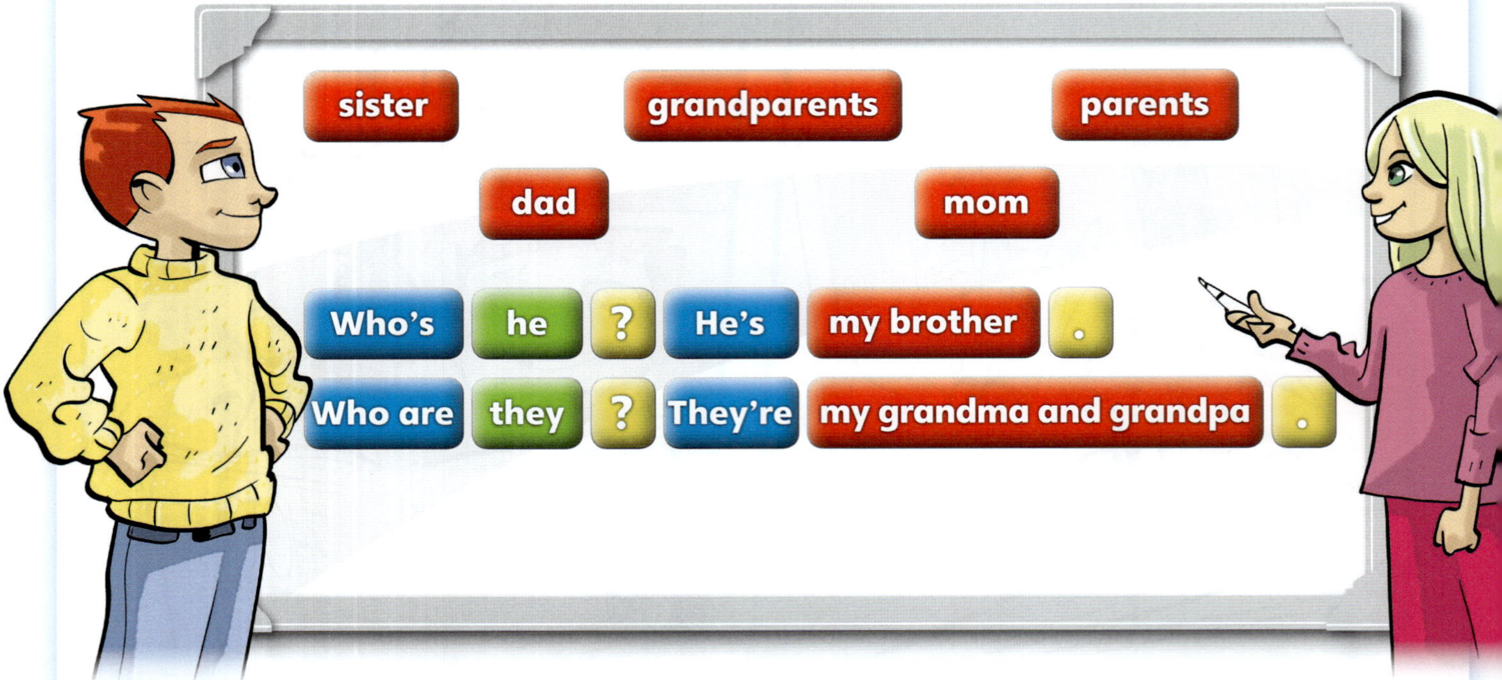

sister   grandparents   parents

dad   mom

Who's | he | ? | He's | my brother | .

Who are | they | ? | They're | my grandma and grandpa | .

10 Follow. Then draw and say.

1 Who's he?

2 Who's she?

3 Who are they?

4 Who are they?

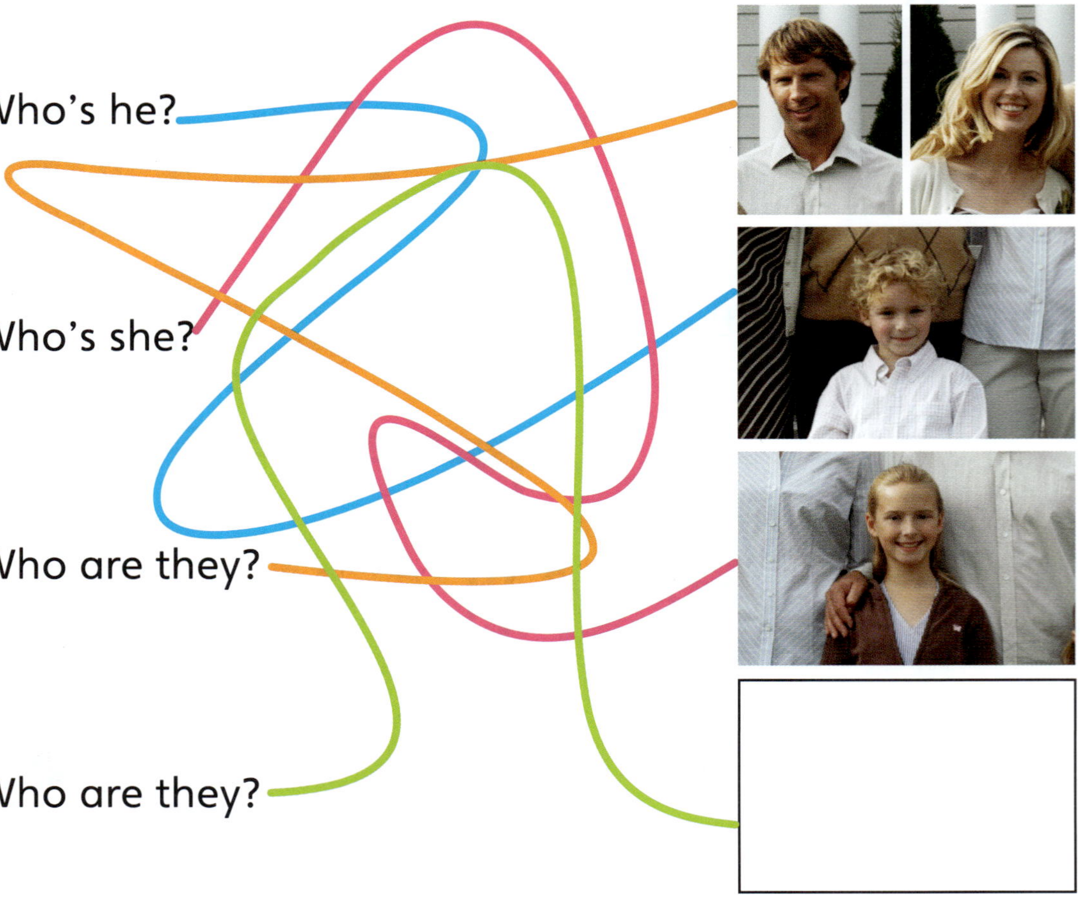

30 Unit 2 language practice (*Who's she? She's my sister.*)

Language in Action

 Listen and stick. Then say.

1  2

3   4

12 Look at 11. Role-play with a partner.

 How many brothers and sisters do you have?

I have two sisters.

You're number...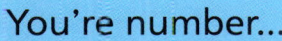

13 Draw and say.

language practice (*How many brothers do you have? I have two brothers.*) Unit 2

Content Connection | Social Science

14 Look, listen, and repeat. Then say.

1 boy   2 girl   3 man   4 woman

> This is a boy. He's my brother.

15 Listen, read, and point. Is the baby a boy or a girl?

This is a picture of my family. Look at the boys. They're my brothers. The girl is my friend. She's my best friend. Her name's Mia. This man is my dad. This is my mom, and the baby is my baby sister! Her name's Anna. This woman is my grandma. I love my family!

THINK BIG Is your teacher a man or a woman? Is your best friend a boy or a girl?

16 **Look at 15. Circle T for true and F for false.**

1 I have one brother. T F
2 The girl is my best friend. T F
3 My dad is a boy. T F
4 I have a baby sister. T F
5 Anna is a woman. T F
6 Mia is my best friend. T F

17 **Draw your family. Then ask and answer.**

Who's this?

This is my brother.

PROJECT

18 **Make a Family poster. Then present it to the class.**

My Family

This man is my dad, and this woman is my mom.

content connection (gender) Unit 2

Grammar

19 **Look, listen, and repeat.**

This is my photo album. These are my family pictures.

1 These are my parents. This is my dad, and this is my mom.

2 These are my grandparents. This is my grandpa, and this is my grandma.

3 This is my sister, Sandra. This is me. My name's Mike.

4 These are my brothers. I have three! This is Andy, this is Sam, and this is Jason.

🧍	🧍🧍
This is my dad.	These are my parents.
This is my mom.	These are my grandparents.
This is my sister.	These are my brothers.

20 **Read and match.**

1 my sisters.
3 my brother.
5 my mom.

This is
These are

2 my grandpa.
4 my parents.
6 my grandparents.

34 Unit 2

Grammar

21 **Read and find.**

This is my family. Look at my grandma. Her name's Anne. This is my grandpa. His name's Bob.

The woman is my mom. Her name's Emma. This is my dad. His name's Joe.

I have a brother and a sister. His name's Pete, and her name's Megan.

This is me. My name's Amy.

This is me.	My name's Amy.
This is my brother.	His name's Pete.
This is my sister.	Her name's Megan.

22 **Read and circle.**

1 This is my brother. **Her / His** name's Thomas.

2 This is my mom. **Her / My** name's Penny.

3 This is my baby sister. **My / Her** name's Sharon.

4 This is my grandma. **My / Her** name's Betty.

5 This is my sister. **His / Her** name's Katie.

6 This is my dad. **His / My** name's Paul.

grammar (*This is my dad. These are my brothers.*) Unit 2

Culture Connection | Around the World

23 Look, listen, and repeat. Then say.

Family and Friends

1
2
3

> Who's she? She's Maria. She's from Mexico.

24 Listen and read. Then write the names.

1. Maria is a girl. She's my friend. She's my best friend. She's from Mexico.
2. Minjoon is my friend, too. He's a boy. He's seven. He's from South Korea.
3. My sister is ten. I love my sister. Her name's Celine. She's from France. I'm from France, too!
4. I love my family, and I love my friends, too.

Family	Friends

25 **Look at 24. Read and circle.**

1 Minjoon is a **boy / girl**.
2 Maria is my **friend / best friend**.
3 My sister's name is **Maria / Celine**.
4 Minjoon and Maria are my **family / friends**.
5 Celine is my **best friend / sister**.

26 **Read, circle, and write. Then draw.**

My best friend is a **boy / girl**. **His / Her** name is _____.

This is my **brother / sister / mom / dad**. **His / Her** name is _____.

How many friends do you have?
Do you have a best friend?
What's his/her name?

Values | Help your family.

 27 Listen and read. Then circle.

1 Pam helps her **brother** / **sister**.

2 Tommy helps his **brother** / **sister**.

28 Can you help? Role-play with a partner.

THINK BIG Can you help your family? Can you help more?

38 Unit 2 values

i, s, b, d | **Phonics**

29 **Listen, look, and repeat.**

1 **i** 2 **s** 3 **b** 4 **d**

30 **Listen and find. Then say.**

 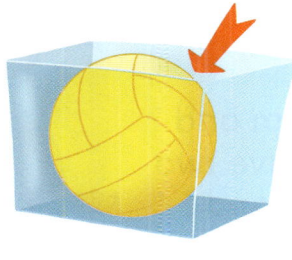  

sit **i**n **d**ad **b**at

31 **Listen and blend the sounds.**

1 i-s is 2 p-i-n pin 3 b-a-d bad
4 d-i-p dip 5 s-a-d sad 6 i-t it

32 **Underline *i*, *s*, *b*, and *d*. Then listen and chant.**

Don't sit, sit, sit
On a pin, pin, pin.
It's bad, bad, bad
To sit on a pin!

phonics (*i, s, b, d*) Unit 2

Review

33 **Work with a partner. Ask and answer. Then draw.**

34 **Play a game.**

Review

 **Listen and ✔.**

1 a  b    2 a  b

3 a  b    4 a  b

36 Listen and number.

a  b  c

I Can
- talk about my family.
- say how many brothers and sisters I have.
- ask to help my family.

review/self-assessment Unit 2 41

unit 3 My Body

1 Listen, look, and say.

1. head
2. eye
3. ear
4. nose
5. mouth
6. neck
7. hand
8. arm
9. finger
10. leg
11. foot
12. toe

2 Listen, find, and say.   **3** Play a game.

4 Listen and sing. Then look at 1 and find.

My Body Song

Do you have two ears?
Do you have one mouth?
Do you have two eyes?
Yes, I do. Yes, I do.

I have ten fingers.
I have ten toes.
I have two feet
And one big nose!

And do you have long legs?
And do you have short hair?
And do you have small hands?
I sing my body song, my body song,
I sing my body song again!

5 Listen and ✓.

1 a b
2 a b
3 a b

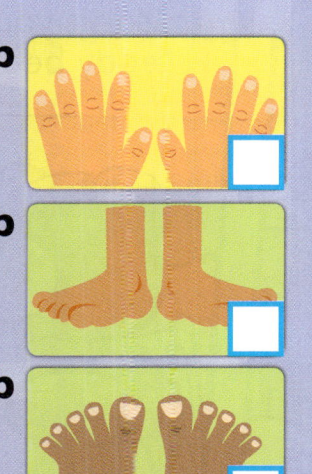

6 Look at 5. Ask and answer.

How many ears do you have?

I have two ears.

THINK BIG Do you have short or long hair? Who do you know who has short or long hair?

song/vocabulary Unit 3   43

Story

7 Listen and read. What's the teddy bear's name?

5. Brown? Oh! Does he have one eye?
Yes, he does! Bobo has one eye!

6. Aha! Is this Bobo?
Yes, it is! Bobo!
Thank you!

8 **Look at the story. Circle Bobo.**

1 a  b 
2 a  b 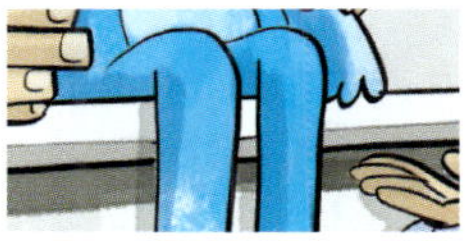
3 a  b

THINK BIG What's your favorite toy? What does it look like? Draw and say.

Language in Action

 9 **Listen. Help Tim and Jane make sentences.**

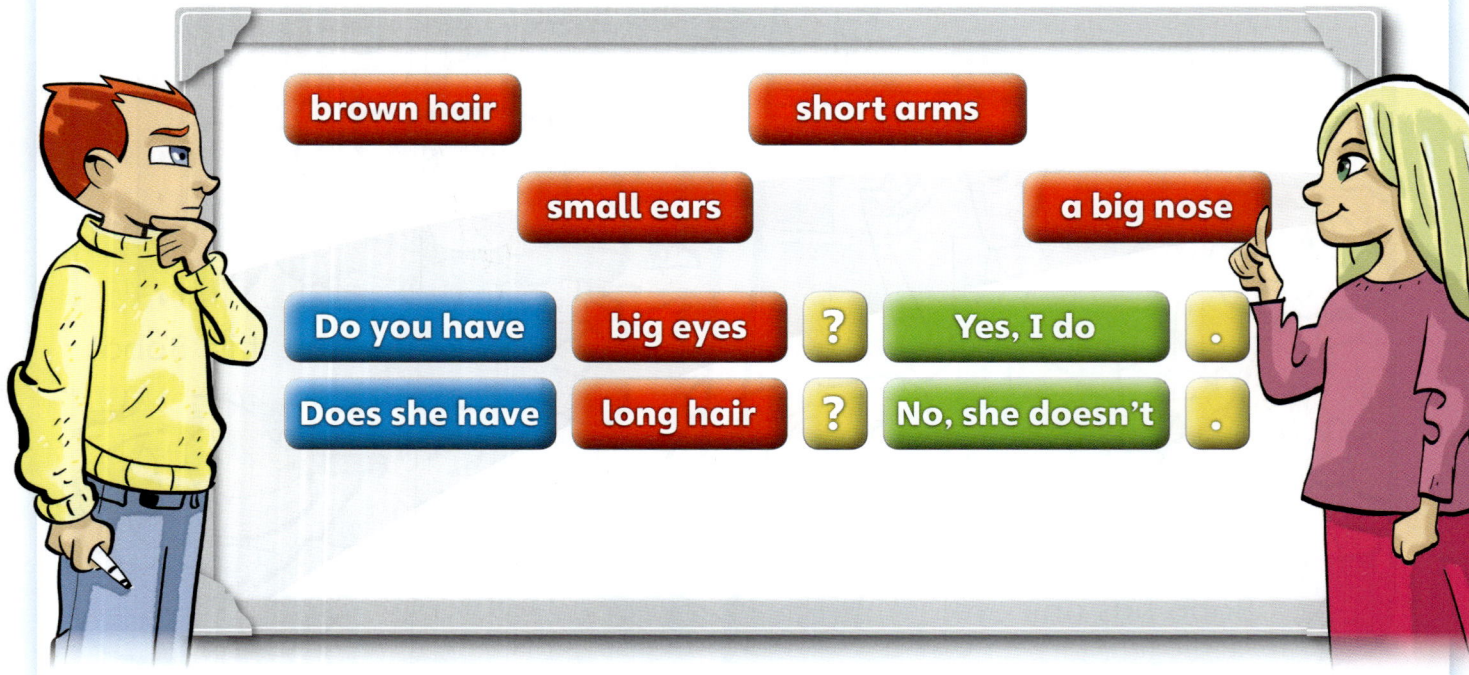

10 **Read and circle. Draw and say.**

1 Does she have short hair?
Yes, she does. / No, she doesn't.

2 Does he have long legs?
Yes, he does. / No, he doesn't.

3 Does it have small ears?
Yes, it does. / No, it doesn't.

4 Does your grandpa have white hair?
Yes, he does. / No, he doesn't.

Content Connection | Science

 Look, listen, and repeat.

1 see   2 smell   3 taste   4 hear

 Look, listen, and read. Then match. What do you taste with?

1 I have two eyes. I see with my eyes. Look! I see a picture.

2 I have one nose. I smell with my nose. I smell a flower.

3 I have one mouth. I taste with my mouth. Mmm! I taste cake!

4 I have two ears. I hear with my ears. Listen! I hear a guitar.

a  picture

b  cake

c  guitar

d  flower

 Can you see, hear, taste, or smell these things?

16 **Look at 15. Circle T for true and F for false. Correct the false sentences.**

1 I taste ice cream with my nose.   T   F
2 I see pictures with my eyes.   T   F
3 I taste cake with my ears.   T   F
4 I hear a guitar with my ears.   T   F
5 I smell flowers with my eyes.   T   F
6 I see a toy with my eyes.   T   F

I taste ice cream with my mouth.

17 **Draw and say.**

1 I see

2 I smell

cake   flower   guitar
ice cream   picture   song
star   teddy bear   TV

3 I taste

4 I hear

I see with my eyes. I see a star.

PROJECT

18 **Make a My Senses poster. Then present it to the class.**

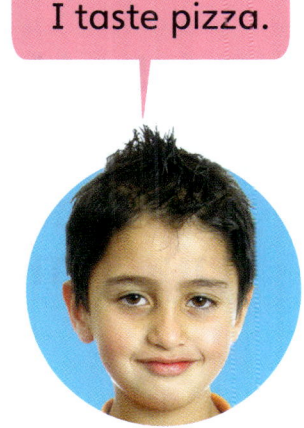

I taste pizza.

Grammar

19 Look, listen, and repeat.

1. It's a chair. — No.
   It's a desk. — Yes!

2. It's an egg. — No.
   It's an eraser. — Yes!

3. They're pencils. — No.
   They're crayons. — Yes!

It's a...	It's an...	They're...
It's a chair.	It's an egg.	They're pencils.
It's a desk.	It's an eraser.	They're crayons.

20 Read and circle.

1 It's a / **It's an** apple.
2 It's a / **They're** rectangles.
3 **It's a** / It's an circle.
4 It's a / **It's an** orange.
5 It's a / **They're** notebooks.
6 **It's a** / They're foot.

Grammar

21 Look and read. Put a ✔ or a ✘ in the box.

1 They're hands. ☐

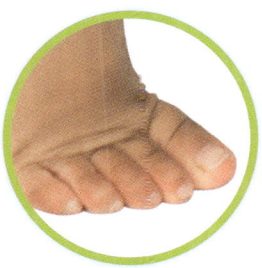
2 They're toes. ☐

3 It's a finger. ☐

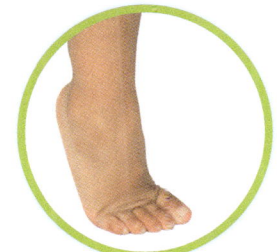
4 It's a foot. ☐

22 Read and match.

apple.   balls.   **It's a**   markers.   orange.

box.   pens.   square.
         chairs.   **It's an**
         egg.   eraser.
circle.
         insect.   **They're**   triangle.
                                                            ear.

23 Look around your classroom. Point and say with a partner.

They're desks.

It's a computer.

grammar (*It's a chair. It's an egg. They're pencils.*) Unit 3 **51**

Culture Connection | Around the World

24 Look and say. What other colors do you know?

Flags of All Colors

yellow orange purple black white brown

25 Listen and read. Then match and say.

1   Brazil has a green, yellow, and blue flag.

2   The green, white, and orange flag is from Ireland.

3   South Africa has a red, green, yellow, blue, black, and white flag.

4   The flag from France is blue, white, and red.

a

b

c

d

Ireland?   Green, white, and orange.

52 Unit 3

26 **Look at 25. Read and circle.**

1 This flag is green, white, and orange.　　**France / Ireland**
2 This flag is blue, green, and yellow.　　**Brazil / France**
3 This flag is blue, yellow, and black.　　**South Africa / Brazil**
4 This flag is blue, white, and red.　　**France / Ireland**

27 **Look at 25. Ask and answer.**

 How many flags have green?

 Three.

28 **Draw and color your country's flag. Then talk with a partner.**

Where are you from?

I'm from France.

What color is your flag?

It's red, white, and blue.

THINK BIG How many colors does your country's flag have? Whose flag has the most colors?

culture connection (flags) Unit 3

Values | Keep clean.

 29 Listen and number. Then listen and repeat.

Rinse with water.   Dry your hands.   Wash with soap.

 30 Listen and circle. Then match and sing.

Keep Clean

1. Every day
   Before I eat
   And after I play,
   I **dry** / **wash** my hands.

2. With a lot of soap
   It's easy, you see.
   Rinse / **Dry** with water
   Just like me.

3. **Dry** / **Wash** them well and
   Sing this song.
   Keep your hands clean
   All day long!

a

b

c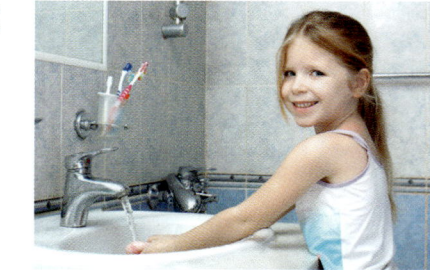

THINK BIG Do you wash your hands before you eat? Why?

e, c, g, m | Phonics

 31 **Listen, look, and repeat.**

1 e   2 c   3 g   4 m

 32 **Listen and find. Then say.**

cap   map   pen   gas

 33 **Listen and blend the sounds.**

1 p-e-t   pet   2 c-a-t   cat   3 g-e-t   get
4 m-a-t   mat   5 w-i-g   wig

 34 **Underline e, c, g, and m. Then listen and chant.**

The cap is on the cat.
The cat goes on the map.
The pen goes on the bed.

Review

 96

35 Complete the monster. Listen, draw, and color.

36 Draw your own monster. Ask and answer with a partner.

 How many heads does it have?

It has three heads!

Review

37 Listen and ✓.

1 a   b

2 a    b

3 a    b

4 a    b

38 Look and write. Use It's a, It's an, and They're.

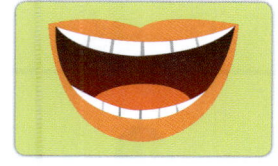 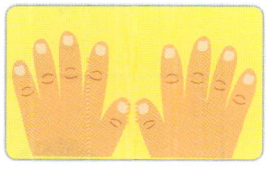 

1 _____   2 _____   3 _____

ear
hands
mouth

I Can

☐ name one or more parts of the body.
☐ talk about my senses.
☐ say how I keep clean.

Checkpoint | Units 1–3

Do I Know It?

1 **Look and circle. Practice.**

😊 I know this.   😟 I don't know this.

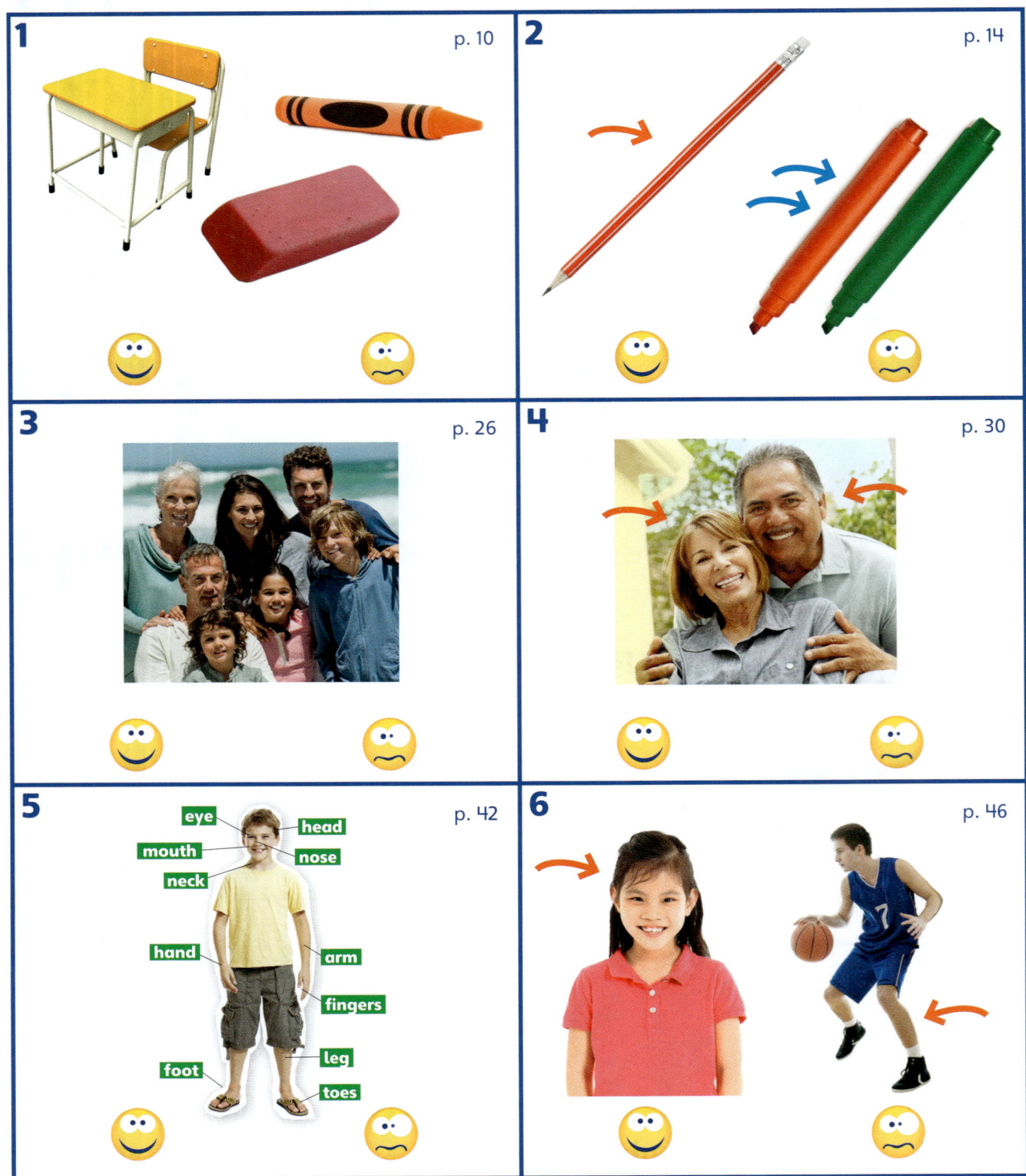

I Can Do It!

2 Get ready.

A Listen and number.

B Look at **A** and point. Ask and answer.

- What is it?
- It's a backpack.

C Listen and circle.

1 Mark

2 Kate

D Look at **C** and point. Role-play with a partner.

- Who's she?
- She's my sister.

Checkpoint | Units 1–3

3 Get set.

 Cut out the cards on page 181.
Now you're ready to **Go!**

4 Go!

A Listen. Put the cards on the numbers.

1	2	3
4	5	6

B Point to a card. Ask and answer.

> Card 2. Does she have long hair?

> Yes, she does.

60 Checkpoint Units 1–3

5 Write and draw.

All About Me

My name is: _____

This is me.

This is my family.

Do I Know It Now?

6 Think about it.

A Go to page **58**. Look and circle again.

B Check (✔).

☐ I can start the next unit.

☐ I can ask my teacher for help and then start the next unit.

☐ I can practice and then start the next unit.

7 Rate this Checkpoint. Color the stars.

easy   hard

fun   not fun

Units 1–3 Exam Preparation

– Part A –

Listen and color. There is one example.

– Part B –

Look and read. Put a check (✓) or a cross (✗) in the box. There are two examples.

Examples

This is a pencil. ✓

This is a book. ✗

Questions

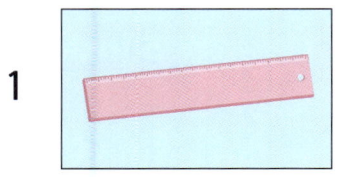

1 This is a ruler. ☐

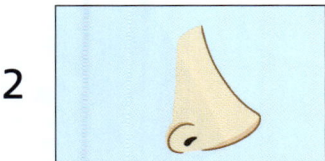

2 This is an eye. ☐

3 This is a grandma. ☐

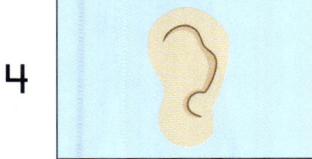

4 This is an ear. ☐

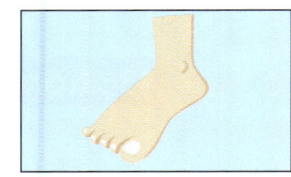

5 This is a leg. ☐

unit 4
My Favorite Clothes

🎧 **1** **Listen, look, and say.**

1 boots
2 dress 
3 gloves 
4 hat 
5 jacket 
6 pants 
7 blouse 
8 shoes 
9 skirt 
10 T-shirt 
11 socks 
12 shirt 
13 shorts 

 2 **Listen, find, and say.**   **3** **Play a game.**

4. Listen and chant. Then look at 1 and find.

What Are You Wearing?

What are you wearing?
I'm wearing a T-shirt.
What are you wearing?
I'm wearing a skirt.

What's he wearing?　　　What's she wearing?
He's wearing new shorts.　She's wearing a red hat.
What's he wearing?　　　What's she wearing?
He's wearing old boots.　She's wearing pink shoes.

5. Listen and number in order.

a 　b 　c 　d

e 　f 　g 　h

6. Point, ask, and answer.

What is it?

It's a pink T-shirt.

THINK BIG Look, think, and say the clothes.

Story

7 Listen and read. What color is Patrick's hat?

8 **Look and match.**

1  2  3  4

a  b  c  d

THINK BIG **Draw a funny hat. Then show the class.**

Language in Action

9 **Listen. Help Tim and Jane make sentences.**

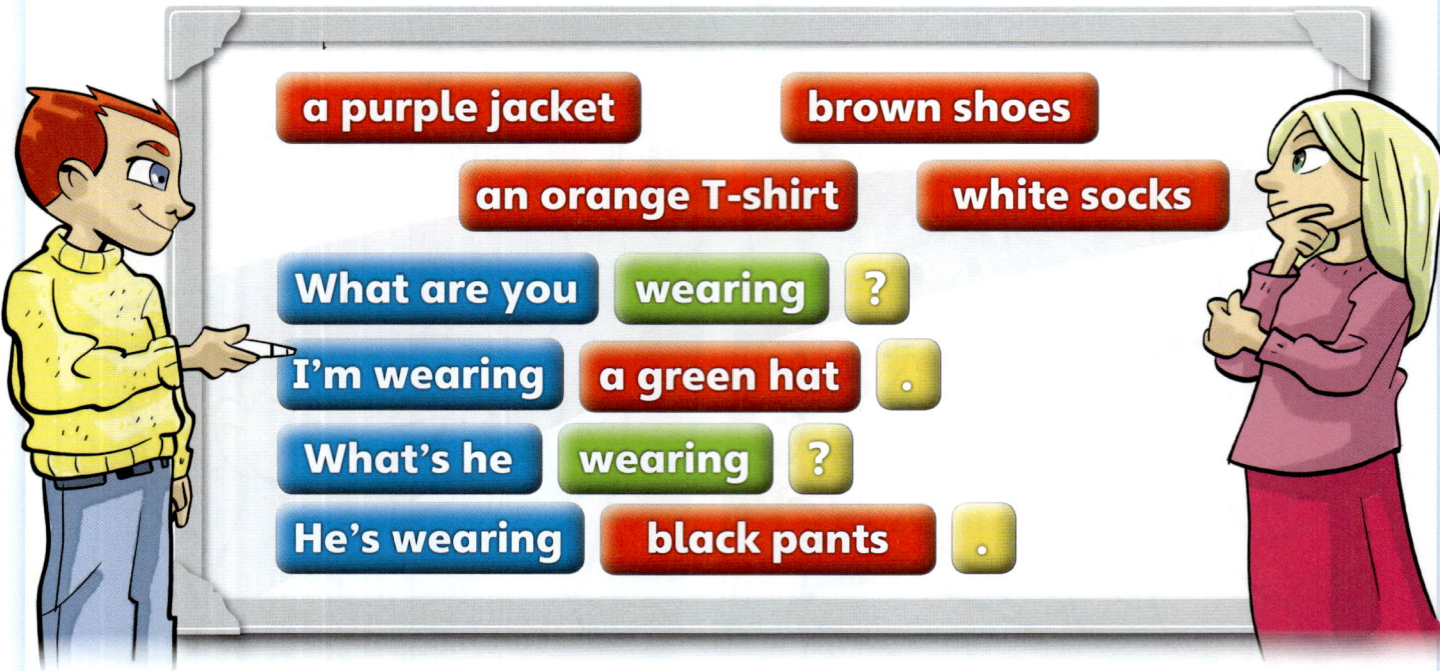

- a purple jacket
- brown shoes
- an orange T-shirt
- white socks

What are you wearing?
I'm wearing a green hat.
What's he wearing?
He's wearing black pants.

10 **Match. Then say. Use He's wearing or She's wearing.**

1 2 3 4

a b c d

Language in Action

11 **Listen and stick. Then say.**

12 **Role-play with a partner.**

What are you wearing?

I'm wearing an orange T-shirt...

13 **What are you wearing? Draw and say.**

language practice (*What are you wearing? I'm wearing an orange shirt.*) Unit 4

Content Connection | Social Science

14 **Look, listen, and repeat. Then say.**

1. hot 2. wet 3. cold 4. dry

5. mountains 6. desert 7. jungle

> It's cold.

> The mountains.

15 **Listen, read, and point. Is it wet in the desert?**

> The weather isn't the same everywhere. It's very cold in the mountains. It isn't hot. He's wearing his hat and gloves. It's very hot and dry in the desert. It isn't cold. She's wearing her shorts and hat. It's wet in the jungle. He's wearing his jacket and boots.

THINK BIG Where is she? Draw and say.

> It's... I'm wearing...

70 Unit 4

16 **Look at 15. Read, circle, and draw. Then say.**

1 It's **hot / cold** in the mountains. I'm wearing 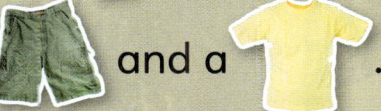 and a .

2 It's **dry / wet** in the desert. I'm wearing 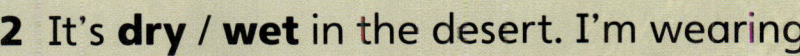 and a .

3 It's **cold / wet** in the jungle. I'm wearing 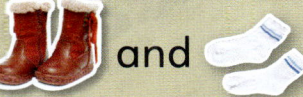 and .

4 It's **hot / cold** and **wet / dry** today. I'm wearing ☐, ☐, and a ☐.

17 **Look at 15. Play a game.**

What are you wearing?

I'm wearing a hat. It's cold.

You're in the mountains.

Yes.

PROJECT

18 **Make a Clothes poster. Then present it to the class.**

My Clothes

It's hot in the jungle. I'm wearing a dress.

Grammar

 19 Look, listen, and point. Then say.

> She's three.

a  b  c

Question	Answer
How old **are you**?	**I'm** seven.
How old **is he**?	**He's** four.
How old **is she**?	**She's** three.
How old **are they**?	**They're** eight.

20 Read and match.

1 How old is Penny? a They're nine.
2 How old are you? b He's ten.
3 How old are Pete and Max? c She's six.
4 How old is Jimmy? d I'm eight.

21 Read and write.

> He's   I'm   She's   They're

1 How old is she? _____ six.
2 How old are they? _____ seven.
3 How old is he? _____ nine.
4 How old are you? _____ ten.

Grammar

22 **Read, circle, and find. Then say.**

1 How old **are you** / **are they**?

2 How old **is he** / **is she**?

3 How old **are they** / **are you**?

4 How old **is she** / **is he**?

- 8
- 4
- 10
- 6

23 **Read and circle. Then match and say.**

Today is my birthday. **Are you** / **I'm** nine. Jenny is my sister. **He's** / **She's** five. She's a little girl. I have a baby brother. **He's** / **She's** one. Johnny is my best friend. **He's** / **She's** nine, too! My grandparents are 70. They're very old!

1 How old are you?
2 How old is your brother?
3 How old is your sister?
4 How old are your grandparents?

1   5
70
9

24 **Draw yourself. Then write.**

This is me. I'm _____ years old.

Culture Connection | Around the World

25 Look, listen, and number. What hats do you have?

FUNNY HATS!

I have a white cap and a purple wool hat.

26 Listen, read, and point. Why are some hats funny?

1. This is Ascot. It's in England. Many people go and watch the horse races. They also look at the hats women have.

2. Some hats are very big and have many colors. Red, blue, yellow, and green.

3. Some hats have very big flowers or long feathers. They're beautiful.

4. There are some very funny hats, too. They have birds, horses, teacups, and umbrellas on them! Do you wear funny hats?

27 **Look at 26. Read and circle.**

1 People watch the **horse / bird** races at Ascot.
2 Some hats have very big **colors / flowers**.
3 Some hats have long **feathers / birds**.
4 Some hats have many **colors / races**.
5 Some hats are **funny / umbrellas**.
6 There are **women / teacups** on some of the hats.

28 **Draw yourself wearing a funny hat. Then talk with a partner.**

My hat has dogs on it.

What a funny hat!

THINK BIG **When do you wear a funny hat? Tell a friend.**

Values | Respect all cultures.

 29 **Listen and number. Then say.**

a b c

They're wearing traditional clothes from Guatemala.

They're wearing traditional clothes from the Philippines.

They're wearing traditional clothes from Kenya.

 30 **Look at 29. Ask and answer.**

 What are they wearing?

They're wearing big hats and blue dresses.

THINK BIG Do people wear traditional clothes in your country? What do they wear?

76 Unit 4 values

o, k, ck | Phonics

 31 **Listen, look, and repeat.**

1 o   2 k   3 ck

 32 **Listen and find. Then say.**

kid   sock   on

 33 **Listen and blend the sounds.**

1 p-o-t pot   2 k-i-t-e kite   3 n-e-ck neck
4 k-i-ck kick   5 d-o-g dog   6 p-i-ck pick

 34 **Underline o, k, and ck. Then listen and chant.**

Put on your socks,
Put on your shorts.
Kick the ball,
Kick, kick, kick!

phonics (o, k, ck) Unit 4 **77**

Review

35 **Work in two pairs. Ask and answer.**

36 **Work in two groups. One group looks away and answers the teacher. Score 1 point for each correct answer.**

Take turns. Which group remembers the most?

Review

37 **Listen and ✓.**

1 a    b    c

2 a    b    c

3 a    b    c

4 a    b    c

38 **Look and write. Use How old.**

1 _____
_____
They're eight.

2 _____
_____
He's five.

I Can

☐ say what people are wearing and their age.
☐ talk about clothes.
☐ respect all cultures.

Busy at Home

unit 5

1 Listen, look, and say.

1 brushing my teeth

2 drinking

3 combing my hair

4 reading

5 taking a bath

6 making lunch

7 washing

8 getting dressed

9 sleeping

10 playing

11 talking on the phone

12 eating

2 Listen, find, and say.   **3** Play a game.

80   Unit 5 vocabulary (home activities)

4 Listen and sing. Then look at **1** and find.

What Are You Doing?

I'm brushing my teeth.
I'm combing my hair.
I'm busy. I'm busy.
What are you doing?

I'm eating my breakfast.
I'm washing my face.
I'm busy. I'm busy.
What are you doing?

I'm talking on the phone.
I'm making my lunch.
I'm busy. I'm busy.
What are you doing?

Chorus

5 Listen and say **yes** or **no**.

1    2    3

6 Look at **5**. Ask and answer.

> What are you doing?

> I'm eating.

> You're Number 1!

 **Why do we brush our teeth?**
Why do we sleep?

Story

7 Listen and read. What's Patrick drawing?

8 **Look at the story. Circle.**

1 Who is playing?

2 Who is making lunch?

3 Who is drawing?

THINK BIG **Draw a picture for your mom. Say.**

Language in Action

9 Listen. Help Tim and Jane make sentences.

10 Listen and ✔. Then say.

1 What's she doing?
a   b

2 What's he doing?
a   b

3 What's he doing?
a   b

4 What's she doing?
a   b

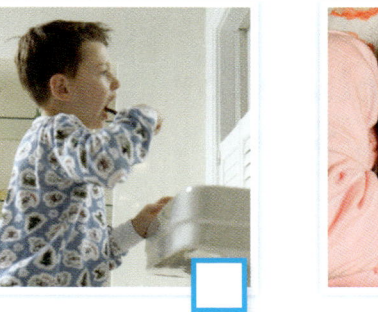

84   Unit 5 language practice (*What are you doing? I'm talking on the phone.*)

Language in Action

11 Listen and stick. Then say.

12 Look at **11**. Ask and answer.

What's she doing?

She's sleeping.

13 Draw yourself and say.

language practice (*What's she doing? She's sleeping.*) Unit 5

Content Connection | Art

14 🎧 139 **Look, listen, and repeat. Then point and say.**

1 apartment   **2 yurt**   **3 houseboat**   **4 lighthouse**

> It's a houseboat.

15 🎧 140 **Look, listen, and read. What shapes are there?**

1. My home is a yurt. It's a circle. It's white and very big. It has a big door.

2. This is my home. It's a houseboat. It has two small windows. They're circles. It has one big window. It's a square.

3. My home is a lighthouse. It's a circle. It has a big door. The door is a rectangle.

4. This is my home. It's an apartment. It's in a tall building. It has big windows. They're rectangles.

THINK BIG Find and draw a picture of one of these houses. What shapes can you see?
a igloo   **b** hut   **c** teepee

16 **Look at 15. Read and match.**

1 My home is a white circle.
   It has two small windows.
2 My home has a big door.
   It's a rectangle.
3 My home has big windows.
   They're rectangles.
4 My home has one big window.
   It's a square.

a houseboat
b apartment
c lighthouse
d yurt

17 **Look at 15. Play a game.**

It has two small windows. They're circles.

Yes.

It's a houseboat.

PROJECT

18 **Make a House Shapes poster. Then present it to the class.**

My house is a square. It has two windows. They're circles. The door is a rectangle.

Grammar

19 **Look, listen, and point. Then say.**

a 　　b

c 　　d

It's small. It's white.

It's...	They're...
It's brown and white.	They're yellow.
It's big.	They're small.
What color is it?	What color are they?

20 **Read and match.**

1 It's brown and white.

2 They're yellow.

3 They're black and brown.

4 It's white.

What color is it?

What color are they?

5 It's pink.

6 They're red and green.

21 **Read and circle.**

1 What color **is it / are they**?　　They're orange and red.

2 What color is it?　　**It's / They're** gray and white.

3 What color are they?　　**It's / They're** pink and blue.

4 What color **is it / are they**?　　It's purple.

Grammar

22 **Look, read, and write.**

| are they | is it | It's | They're |

1 What color is it?
_____ red.

2 What color are they?
_____ blue and yellow.

3 What color _____
_____? It's blue and white.

4 What color _____ _____?
They're red, green, yellow, and blue.

23 **Read and draw.**

The Haunted House.

This is a haunted house. It has three ghosts. They're white. Boo!

The door is tall. It's brown. Bang!

The window is big. The curtains are red. They're long. Whoosh!

The house has a black cat. It's big. It's scary. Meow!

24 **Look around your classroom. Ask and answer with a partner.**

What color is it?

What color are they?

It's white. The desk is white.

They're red and green. The pens are red and green.

grammar (*It's brown and white. They're small.*) Unit 5

Culture Connection | Around the World

25 Is your home an apartment or a house? Talk about it.

Homes

My home is an apartment. It's big. It has five rooms. It has big windows.

26 Listen and read. Where do Mom and Dad sleep?

1. This is my home. It's a motor home. It's in a trailer park.
2. It has a kitchen, but it doesn't have a dining room. The kitchen has a small table. It's a square. The kitchen has four chairs.
3. The living room has a big TV. It's a rectangle.
4. My home has two bedrooms. My mom and dad sleep in the big bedroom. My bedroom is small, but it has a big window.
5. The bathroom is small, too. It has a small window. It's a circle.
6. My motor home isn't very big, but it's very comfortable. My family is happy here.

27 Look at **26**. Read and circle.

1 This is my home. It's **a motor home / an apartment**.
2 It doesn't have a **kitchen / dining room**.
3 The kitchen has four **tables / chairs**.
4 The TV is a **rectangle / square**.
5 Mom and Dad sleep in the **small / big** bedroom.
6 The bathroom has a **small / big** window.

28 Look at **26**. Play a game.

It has a big TV. It's a rectangle.

The living room.

29 Draw a motor home for you. Talk with a partner.

My motor home has a small kitchen and two bedrooms.

 Why do some people live in a motor home? Talk about it.

culture connection (homes) Unit 5   **91**

Values | Help at home.

30 **Listen and match. Then listen and repeat.**

She's helping her parents.   She's cleaning her room.
She's drying the dishes.   He's washing the dishes.

1

2

3

4

31 **How do you help at home? Act it out. Your partner guesses.**

He's drying the dishes.

THINK BIG Does it feel good to help at home? Why?

u, f, ff | Phonics

 32 **Listen, look, and repeat.**

1 u   2 f   3 ff

 33 **Listen and find. Then say.**

fan   up   puff

 34 **Listen and blend the sounds.**

1 r-u-n   run   2 f-u-n   fun   3 o-ff   off
4 s-u-n   sun   5 f-o-g   fog

 35 **Underline u, f, and ff. Then listen and chant.**

We're having fun,
Running in the sun.
Up, up, up!
Puff, puff, puff!

Review

36 **Work in groups. Play the Memory game.**

Student 1: Act and say.

Student 2: Talk about Student 1. Then act and say.

I'm eating.

She's eating. I'm reading.

She's eating. He's reading. I'm washing.

Student 3: Talk about Students 1 and 2. Then act and say.

Play with the whole class. How much can you remember?

Review

37 Listen and number.

a

b

c

d

e

38 Look and match.

1 It's red.　　2 They're white.　　3 It's green.　　4 They're small.

a

b

c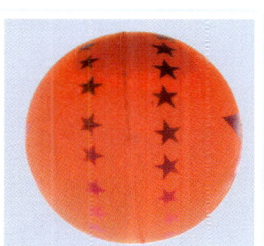

d

I Can

- [ ] talk about home activities.
- [ ] name shapes in homes and describe things.
- [ ] talk about helping at home.

On the Farm

1 Listen, look, and say.

1 cat

2 dog

3 cow

4 sheep

5 turtle

6 horse

7 duck

8 frog

9 chicken

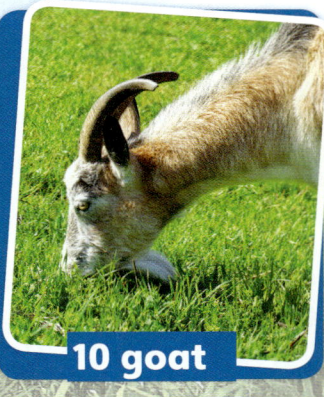
10 goat

2 Listen, find, and say.   **3** Play a game.

4 Listen and chant. Then look at 1 and find.

Look at the Animals

Look over here!
Look over there!
There are animals
Everywhere!

What is it?
It's a duck.
What's it doing?
It's flying up high!

What is it?
It's a dog!
What's it doing?
It's jumping with the frogs!

What are they?
They're goats!
What are they doing?
They're eating some oats!

Chorus

5 Listen and number.

a  b  c

6 Look at 5. Ask and answer.

What is it? — It's a horse.
What's it doing? — It's running.

THINK BIG What animals can jump?
What animals can fly?

Story

7 Listen and read. What's the goat doing?

8 **Look and number.**

1 running **2** flying **3** eating **4** jumping

a  b

c  d

THINK BIG What happens next? Draw.

Language in Action

 9 **Listen. Help Tim and Jane make sentences.**

 **10** **Listen and ✓.**

1 a b  2 a  b

3 a  b  4 a  b

100 Unit 6 language practice (*What are the chickens doing? They're running.*)

Language in Action

11 Listen and stick. Then say.

12 Look at **11**. Ask and answer.

What's the horse doing?

It's eating.

13 Color and say. What are the animals doing?

Content Connection | Social Science

 14 **Look, listen, and repeat. Then match.**

1 chick   2 puppy   3 kitten   4 calf

a It has black ears.   **b** It's black and white.   **c** It has blue eyes.   **d** It's yellow.

15 **Look, listen, and read. How many baby animals are there?**

1 Look at the cows. The big cow is brown. She has a baby cow. A baby cow is called a calf.

2 The big dog is happy. Look at her baby dogs. Baby dogs are called puppies.

3 This chicken is very big. Look at the baby chickens. They're called chicks.

4 Look at the cats. There's one big cat and three baby cats. Baby cats are called kittens.

 **Read and match.**

chick   kitten   puppy   calf

dog   chicken   cow   cat

16 Listen and number. Then say.

a
A baby chicken is called a...

b
A baby dog is called a...

c
A baby cat is called a...

d
A baby cow is called a...

17 Look at **15**. Play a game.

What are baby dogs called?

Baby dogs are called puppies.

PROJECT

18 Make a **Baby Animals** poster. Then present it to the class.

Baby Animals

a kitten

a calf

a puppy

These are my baby animals. I have a kitten, a calf, and a puppy.

content connection (baby animals) Unit 6

Grammar

19 Look, listen, and number.

a

b

c

d

my	This is my dog.	its	This is its mom.
your	Is this your dog?	our	These are our chickens.
his	His name's Patch.	your	These are your animals.
her	Her name's Misha.	their	They're eating their food.

20 Read and match. Then say. Use This is or These are.

1 Pete
2 me
3 Patty
4 Dad, me, and Mom
5 the kitten
6 you and Sally
7 my brothers

a her puppy
b his cat — *This is his cat.*
c our goats
d my turtle
e your chickens
f their kittens
g its mom

104 Unit 6

Grammar

21 **Read and write.** | her   his   my   their   your |

1 She has a tennis ball. It's _____ ball.

2 I have a brother and a sister. They're _____ family.

3 He has a toy spaceship. It's _____ spaceship.

4 They have a pet. It's _____ dog.

5 You have an old car. It's _____ car.

22 **Play a game. Who is it? Take turns.**
A: Describe a person in your class.
B: Listen to A. Who is it?

His hair is very short. His eyes are blue. His T-shirt is black. His shoes are red.

Is it Tom?

Yes, it is.

23 **Circle and write. Then draw.**

This is my class. Our teacher is a **man** / **woman**. **His** / **Her** name's _____.

This is my best friend. **His** / **Her** name's _____.

These are my classmates. **Their** / **Our** names are _____ and _____.

Culture Connection | Around the World

 Do you have a pet? What's its name? What color is it?

Pets

 Listen and read. What colors are the pets?

1  2  3  4

1. I'm Sharon. I'm from Australia. This is my pet hamster. He's brown. His name's Charlie.

2. My name's Reiko. I'm from Japan. I have a pet canary. He's yellow. His name's Tom Bird.

3. Hi. My name's Zack. I'm from the United States. I have a pet snake. She's green. Her name's Samantha.

4. I'm Elina. I'm from Greece. This is my pet mouse. She's very small. She's white. Her name's Zoe.

26 **Look at 25. Read, circle, and write.**

1 Zack has a **mouse** / **snake**. Her name's _____.
2 Sharon has a **hamster** / **canary**. His name's _____.
3 Elina has a **mouse** / **hamster**. Her name's _____.
4 Reiko has a **snake** / **canary**. His name's _____.

27 **Draw a pet for you. Then describe your pet to a partner.**

I'm Juanita. I'm from Mexico. This is my pet cat. She's...

THINK BIG Which animals make good pets? Which animals make bad pets?

culture connection (pets) Unit 6

Values | Be nice to animals.

 **28 Listen and find the picture. Then listen and repeat.**

1 feeding **2** walking

3 brushing **4** playing

 29 Look at 28. Role-play with a partner.

 What are you doing?

I'm feeding the chicks.

THINK BIG How are you nice to animals? Draw.

r, h, j | Phonics

 30 **Listen, look, and repeat.**

  1 r   **2** h   **3** j

 31 **Listen and find. Then say.**

  hat   **j**am   **r**ock

 32 **Listen and blend the sounds.**

  1 r-e-d   red   **2** h-e-n   hen   **3** j-e-t   jet
  4 r-u-n   run   **5** h-u-t   hut   **6** j-o-b   job

 33 **Underline r, h, and j. Then listen and chant.**

A red hen in
A red hat
Is eating red jam.
Run, red hen, run!

phonics (*r, h, j*) Unit 6 **109**

Review

34 **Listen, find, and say. Then role-play.**

1
2
3
4

35 **Work in teams. Role-play. Ask and answer.**

What's the dog doing?

It's jumping.

Review

36 **Look and match.**

a

b

1 eating

2 flying

3 jumping

4 running

c

d

37 **Listen and number.**

a    b    c    d

38 **Read and circle.**

1 This is my dad. **His** / **Her** name's Tom.
2 Emma's here. **Her** / **My** school is closed.
3 These are our dogs. **Our** / **Their** ears are big.
4 I have short hair. **Your** / **My** hair is black.

I Can

- ☐ talk about what animals and baby animals are doing.
- ☐ talk about possessions.
- ☐ say how to be nice to animals.

Checkpoint | Units 4–6

Do I Know It?

1 **Look and circle. Practice.**

😊 I know this.   😟 I don't know this.

I Can Do It!

2 **Get ready.**

A Look. Circle the correct words.

1. Mom is **reading a book** / **eating**.
2. Dad is **washing** / **making lunch**.
3. The cat is **sleeping** / **playing**.
4. The girl is **drinking** / **talking on the phone**.

B Look at **A** and point. Ask and answer.

> What's she wearing?

> She's wearing a green shirt and brown pants.

C Listen and number.

a   b   c   d

Checkpoint | Units 4–6

3 Get set.

STEP 1 Cut out the cards on page 183.

STEP 2 Put the cards on your desk. Mix the cards up. Now you're ready to **Go!**

4 Go!

A Arrange the cards to make the person below. Ask and answer with a partner.

- What's she wearing?
- What's she doing?

B Make 3 more people. Don't show your cards. Describe one of your people. Your partner makes the same person. Show your cards and check.

> He's in the bathroom. He's talking on the phone...

5 Draw.

All About Me

My favorite animal is:

I'm wearing:

Do I Know It Now?

6 Think about it.

A Go to page **112**. Look and circle again.

B Check (✓).

☐ I can start the next unit.

☐ I can ask my teacher for help and then start the next unit.

☐ I can practice and then start the next unit.

7 Rate this Checkpoint. Color the stars.

easy   hard   fun   not fun

Units 4–6 Exam Preparation

– Part A –

182

Look at the pictures. Now listen and check (✓). There is one examp

Which is Sue?

 A ✓
 B ☐
 C ☐

1 What's Tom doing?

 A ☐
 B ☐
 C ☐

2 Which is Mom?

 A ☐
 B ☐
 C ☐

3 What's in his backpack?

 A ☐
 B ☐
 C ☐

4 What's Anna doing?

 A ☐
 B ☐
 C ☐

5 What's Tom wearing?

 A ☐
 B ☐
 C ☐

– Part B –

Look at the pictures. Look at the letters. Write the words.

Example

   c a t   t c a

Questions

1    _ _ _   o w c

2    _ _ _ _   g d o

3    _ _ _ _   a t o g

4    _ _ _ _   o r f g

5    _ _ _ _ _ _ l e t u t r

Reading and Writing part 3   **117**

unit 7 — Party Time

1 Listen, look, and say.

1 cake
2 fruit
3 ice cream
4 juice
5 milk
6 water
7 pizza
8 salad
9 chicken
10 fries
11 pasta

2 Listen, find, and say. **3** Play a game.

4 Listen and sing. Then look at 1 and find.

It's My Party!

Welcome, friends.
Please sit down.
It's time for my party!
With games and a clown!

I have pizza, chicken,
Salad, too.
Fruit, cake,
And ice cream for you!

Or put some pasta
On your plate.
With juice or milk
It sure tastes great.

Thanks for the presents.
What a great day!
Let's eat and drink
And play, play, play. (x2)

5 Listen and say yes or no.

1    2    3    4

6 Look at 5. Ask and answer.

What does he have?

He has milk.

THINK BIG What food do you eat every day?
What food do you eat on special days?

Story

7 Listen and read. What day is Tim's party?

8 Look at the story. Read and circle.

1 Tim has...

2 Jane has...

3 What does Patrick have?

THINK BIG What day is it today? Circle and say.

Sunday Monday Tuesday Wednesday Thursday Friday Saturday

Language in Action

 9 **Listen. Help Tim and Jane make sentences.**

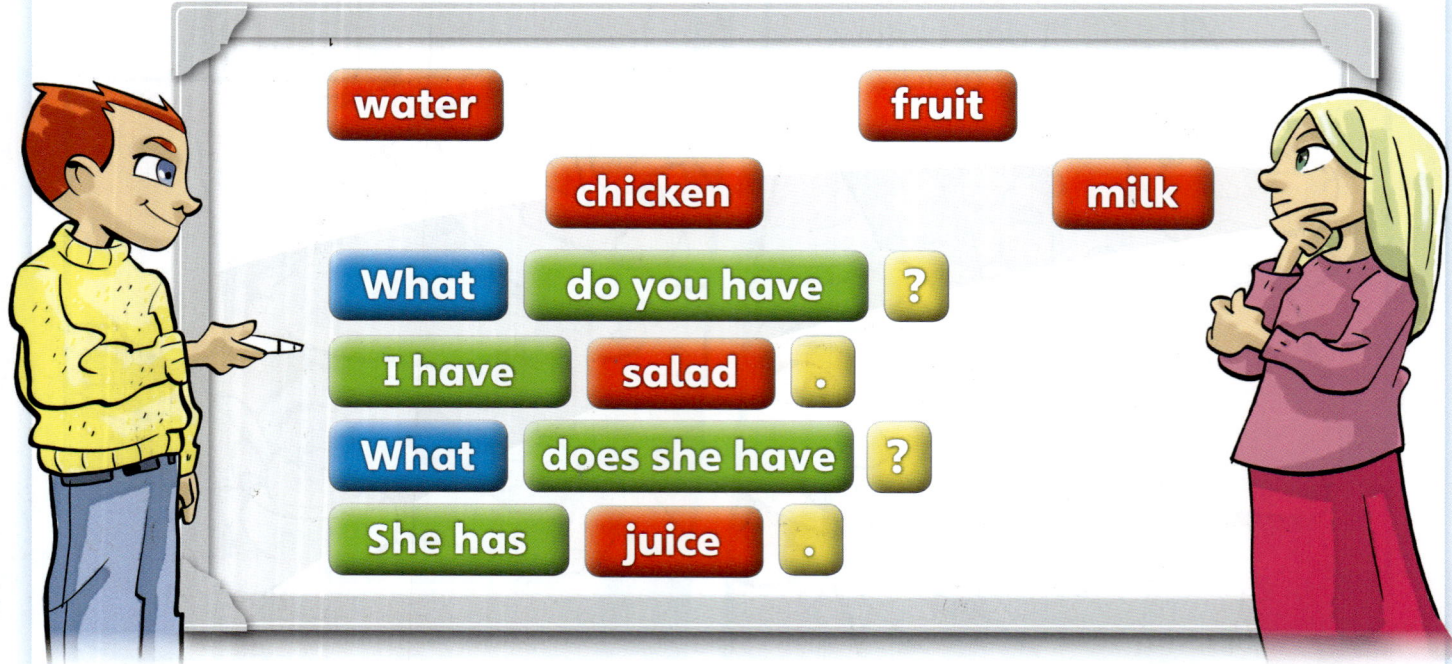

10 **Match. Then say.**

1. What do you have?
   I have salad.

2. What do you have?
   I have cake and milk.

3. What do you have?
   I have juice and ice cream.

4. What do you have?
   I have fruit.

Language in Action

11 🎧 **Listen and stick. Then say.**

1 2
3 4

12 **Look at 11. Ask and answer.**

 What does she have?

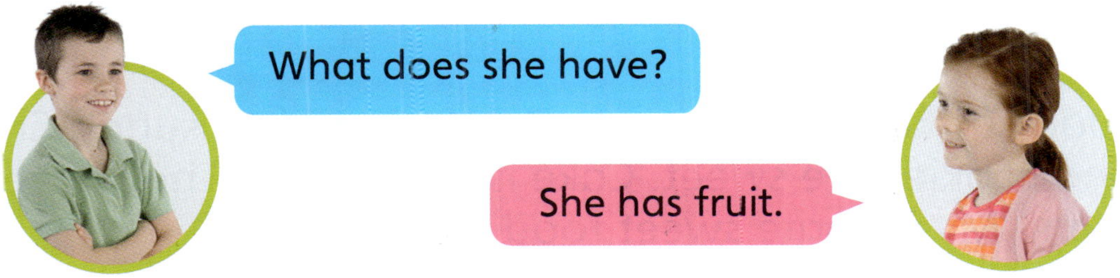

She has fruit.

13 **What do you have? Draw and say.**

language practice (*What does she have? She has fruit.*) Unit 7

Content Connection | Science

 14 **Look, listen, and repeat. Then say.**

1 sugar

2 chocolate

3 cookies

4 salt

5 chips

6 fries

> I have chocolate and fries.

 15 **Listen, read, and point. Is pizza sweet? Is cake salty?**

1. Food can be sweet or salty. Sweet food has sugar. Chocolate and cookies are sweet. Cake is sweet, too. They have sugar in them. My favorite sweet food is chocolate.

2. Chips have salt. Pizza and fries have salt, too. They're all salty. My favorite salty food is pizza.

 **Name other sweet and salty foods. What's your favorite? Salty or sweet?**

16 Look at **15**. Circle **T** for true and **F** for false.

1. Chocolate is sweet.   T   F
2. Cookies are salty.   T   F
3. Chips are salty.   T   F
4. Fries are sweet.   T   F
5. Cake is sweet.   T   F

17 Look and match. Then listen and check.

PROJECT

18 Make a **Sweet and Salty Food** poster. Then present it to the class.

This is my food poster. Chocolate is sweet. Fries are salty.

Grammar

 19 Look, listen, and read. Then say.

1 I don't go to school on Sunday. I don't get up early.

2 My mom doesn't go to work. She doesn't clean the house every day.

3 My dad doesn't go to work. He doesn't watch TV all day.

4 My big sisters don't go to school. They don't study all afternoon.

5 The dog doesn't sleep in its basket. It doesn't let me sleep!

> She doesn't go to school.

I/You/We/They		
I		go to school.
You	don't	do your homework.
We		eat cake.
They		study all afternoon.

He/She/It		
He		sleep in a chair.
She	doesn't	go to work.
It		let me sleep.

Grammar

20 **Read and circle.**

1 I **doesn't** / **don't** drink juice.
2 He **don't** / **doesn't** watch TV in bed.
3 We **don't** / **doesn't** listen to music in class.
4 They **doesn't** / **don't** eat in the car.
5 She **doesn't** / **don't** take a bath in her bedroom.
6 You **don't** / **do** sleep on your desk.

21 **Read and write don't or doesn't.**

1 Paul _____ run in class.
2 Mike and Pete _____ drink juice for lunch.
3 Tony and Sally _____ have a baby brother.
4 The girls _____ wear pants in school.
5 Alex and I _____ walk to school.
6 My brother _____ eat salad.

22 **Make three silly sentences. Tell your partner.**

I sing with my toes.

You don't sing with your toes.

Culture Connection | **Around the World**

23 What food do you have on your birthday? What's your favorite?

Birthday Food

My favorite food is pizza.

24 Listen and read. What food do the children have on their birthdays?

Mexico

1. My name's Miguel. In Mexico, I have a piñata with candy on my birthday. It's my favorite day.

2. I'm Jack. I live in the United States. I have a big cake on my birthday. It's very sweet.

United States

3. I'm Susie from South Korea. I have seaweed soup on my birthday. It's salty.

Korea

4. I'm Anya. I'm from Russia. On my birthday, I have a big fruit pie. It's my favorite sweet cake.

Russia

25 Look at **24**. Read and write.

cake   candy   pie   soup

1 _____   2 _____   3 _____   4 _____

26 Look at **24**. Read and circle. Then say.

1 Miguel doesn't have **cake / candy**.
2 Jack doesn't have **soup / cake**.
3 Susie doesn't have **pie / soup**.
4 Anya doesn't have **cake / pie**.

27 Write about you. Then tell a partner.

My name's _____. On my birthday, I have _____, _____, and _____.

THINK BIG Why do people have special food on their birthday? How else do they celebrate?

culture connection (special food) Unit 7

Values | Eat three meals a day.

28 Look and number in order. Then listen and check.

a
b
c

I eat lunch every day.

I eat dinner every day.

I eat breakfast every day.

29 Read and match. Then draw and say.

1 My brother eats salad for lunch every day.

2 Mom drinks milk for breakfast every day.

3 Dad eats chicken for dinner every day.

4 I eat…

a

b

c

d

THINK BIG Do you eat three meals every day? Why do you think it is important?

l, ll, v, w | Phonics

30 Listen, look, and repeat.

1 l 2 ll 3 v 4 w

31 Listen and find. Then say.

web doll leg van

32 Listen and blend the sounds.

1 l-e-t   let
2 b-e-ll bell
3 v-e-t   vet
4 w-e   we
5 w-i-n   win
6 t-a-ll tall

33 Underline l, ll, v, and w. Then listen and chant.

Let's ring the bell
For the vet
With the van!

Review

 34 Find the differences and say. Then listen and check.

Picture A

Picture B

35 Look at **34**. Play a game.

 In Picture A, Sam has ice cream.

In Picture B, Sam has fruit.

Review

 36 **Listen and circle.**

1 a    b    c

2 a    b    c

3 a    b    c

4 a    b 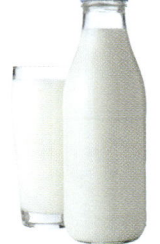   c

37 **Read and circle.**

1 She **doesn't** / **don't** walk to school.
2 They **doesn't** / **don't** eat cookies.
3 I **doesn't** / **don't** play with puppets.
4 We **don't** / **doesn't** like basketball.

I Can

☐ talk about party food.
☐ ask and answer about what people have.
☐ name sweet and salty food.

unit 8 Fun and Games

1 Listen, look, and say.

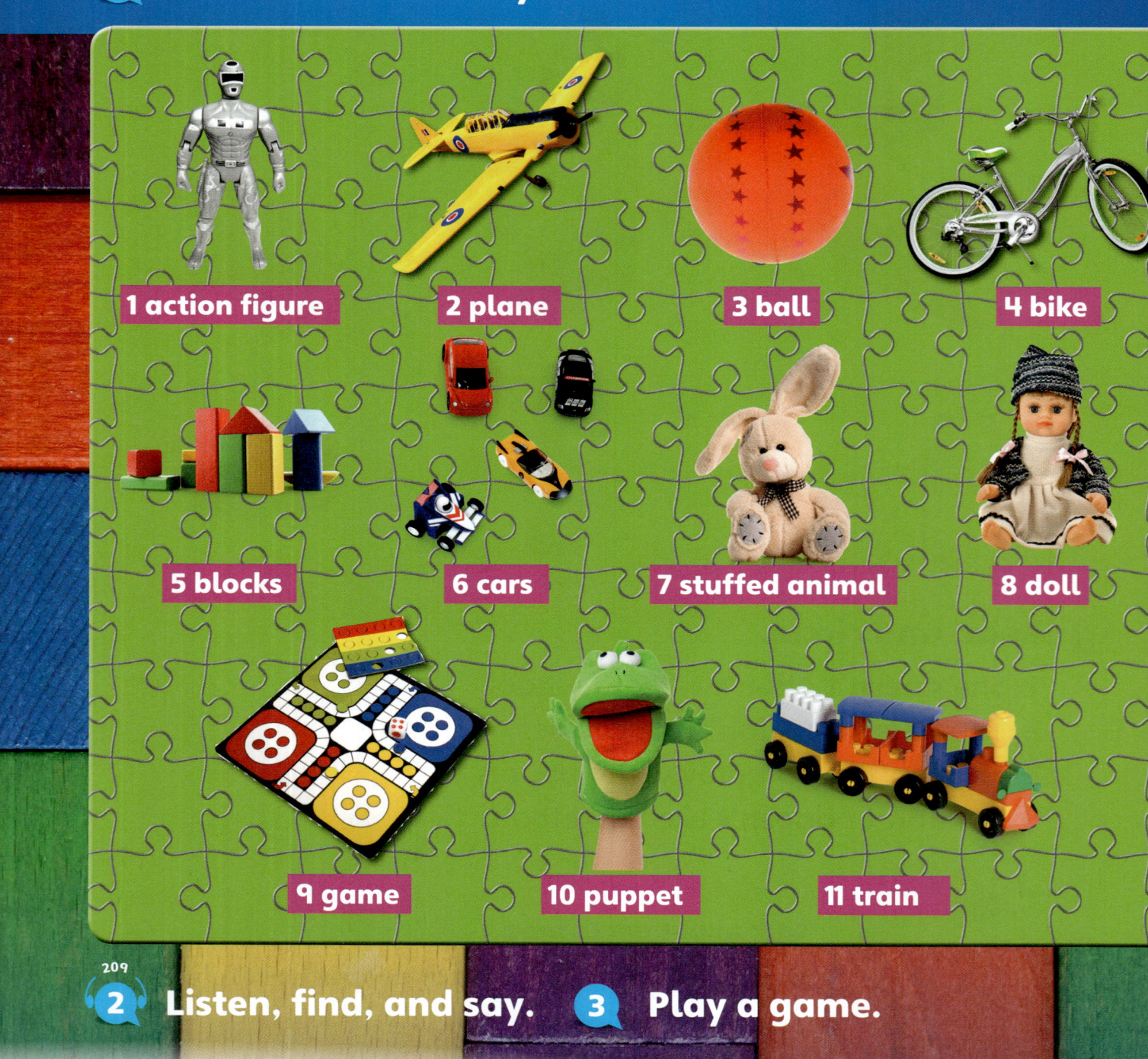

1 action figure
2 plane
3 ball
4 bike
5 blocks
6 cars
7 stuffed animal
8 doll
9 game
10 puppet
11 train

2 Listen, find, and say.   **3** Play a game.

4 Listen and sing. Then look at 1 and find.

What's in Your Toy Box?

Kim, what's in your toy box?
Do you have a plane?
No, but this is my blue car.
And where's my gray train?

Kim, what's on your toy shelf?
Do you have a ball?
Yes, yes, here it is.
And here's my purple doll.

Kim, what's on your table?
Do you have big blocks?
Yes, and these are my puppets.
My favorite's Mr. Fox!

These are my favorite toys,
Purple, green, and gray.
I share my toys with my friends.
And I play every day!

5 Listen and number.

a   b   c

6 Look at 5. Ask and answer.

What's in your toy box?

These are my blocks.

THINK BIG What toys can a baby play with? Why?
What toys can big children play with? Why?

Story

7 Listen and read. Where is Jane's doll?

8 **Look at the story and circle.**

1 Jane's doll is under the  .

2 Jane's action figures are on the .

3 Jane is playing with her 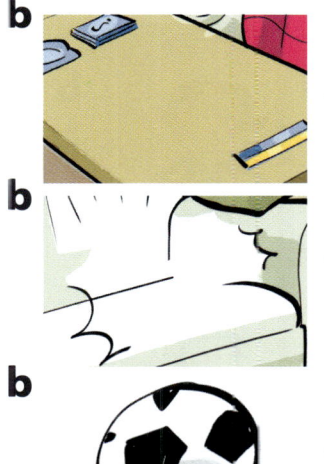 .

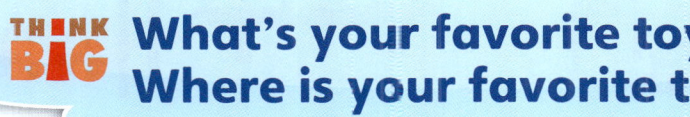
THINK BIG What's your favorite toy? Where is your favorite toy?

Language in Action

9 **Listen. Help Tim and Jane make sentences.**

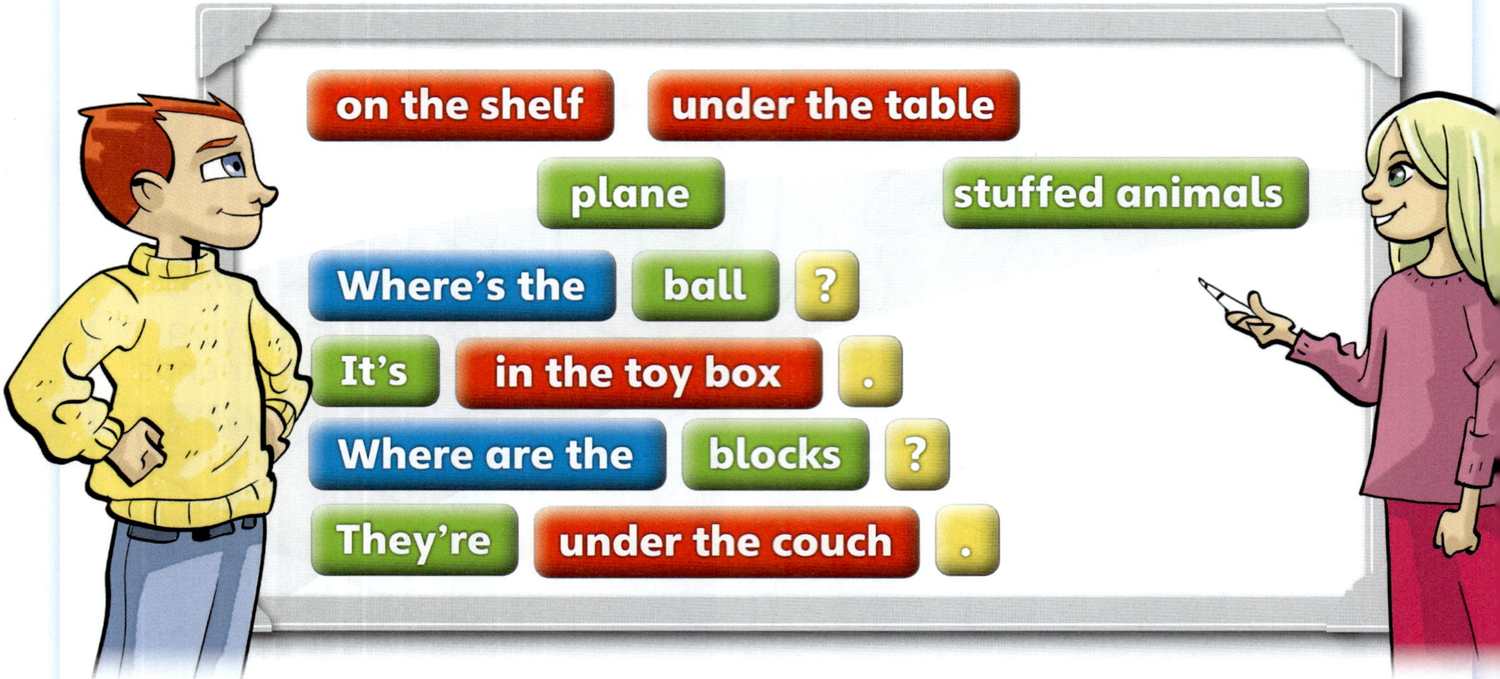

on the shelf   under the table   plane   stuffed animals

Where's the ball?
It's in the toy box.
Where are the blocks?
They're under the couch.

10 **Listen and ✓.**

1 a   b

2 a   b

3 a   b

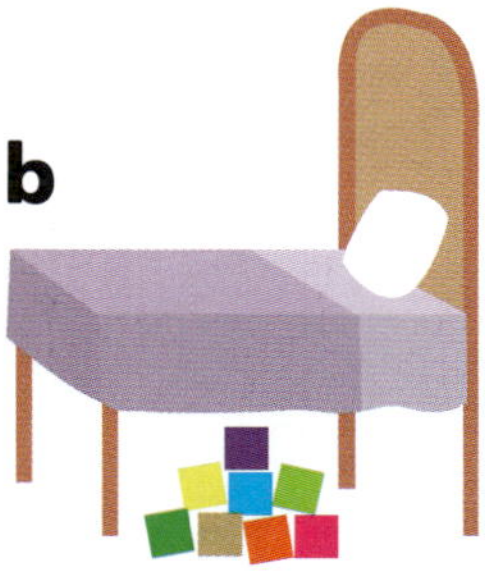

4 a   b

138 Unit 8 language practice (*Where's the ball? It's in the toy box.*)

Language in Action

11 **Listen and stick. Then say.**

 **12** **Look at 11. Ask and answer.**

Where are the dolls?

They're under the table.

13 **Color and say. Where are the toys?**

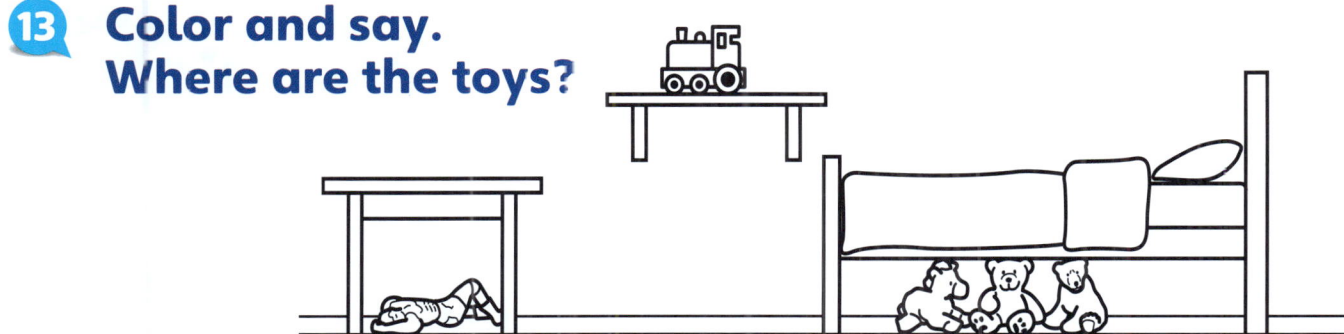

language practice (*Where are the dolls? They're under the table.*) Unit 8

Content Connection | Art

14 Do you have a kite? What does it look like?

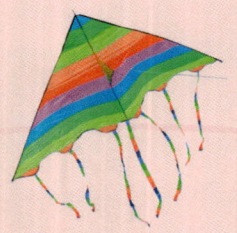 

I have a kite. My kite is big. It's colorful.

15 Look, listen, and read. Then match.

There are many kite flying festivals in Japan. The kites look like different animals. People fly their kites high in the sky. The best kite wins. Let's look at some.

1 This kite looks like a dragon.
It's red, black, and yellow.
It's long and colorful.

a

2 This kite looks like a bird.
It's blue and orange.
It's high in the sky.

b

3 This kite looks like a butterfly.
It's green. It's very big.

c

4 This kite looks like a fish.
It's orange. It has a long tail.

d

THINK BIG Find a picture of a kite. What color is it? What does it look like?

140 Unit 8

16 **Look at 15. Read and write.**

| big bird red fish |

1 This kite looks like a butterfly. It's green. It's very _____.
2 This kite looks like a _____. It's orange. It has a long tail.
3 This kite looks like a dragon. It's _____, black, and yellow. It's long and colorful.
4 This kite looks like a _____. It's blue and orange. It's high in the sky.

17 **Look at 15. Play a game.**

It's orange. It has a long tail.

Picture c. The fish kite.

PROJECT

18 **Make a Cool Kite. Then present it to the class.**

This is my kite. It looks like a fish. It's yellow. It has a long tail.

Grammar

19 **Look, listen, and point. Then say.**

There is salad.

There are sandwiches.

There's a pizza.	There are sandwiches.
There isn't a cake.	There aren't fries.
Is there a salad?	Are there sandwiches?
Yes, there is. No, there isn't.	Yes, there are. No, there aren't.

20 Read and circle.

1 There **is** / **are** ten books on the shelf.
2 There **is** / **are** eight cats in the basket.
3 There **is** / **are** a ball under the couch.
4 There **is** / **are** a shoe on the bed.
5 There **is** / **are** twelve cars in the toy box.
6 There **is** / **are** a marker on the desk.

Grammar

21 Look and ✔.

1 Are there balls? Yes, there are. ☐ No, there aren't. ☐
2 Is there an action figure? Yes, there is. ☐ Yes, there are. ☐
3 Is there a stuffed animal? No, there aren't. ☐ Yes, there is. ☐
4 Are there cars? No, there aren't. ☐ Yes, there are. ☐
5 Is there an airplane? Yes, there is. ☐ No, there isn't. ☐
6 Are there skates? No, there isn't. ☐ Yes, there are. ☐

22 Read and match.

1 Is there a   a egg in the box?
2 Are there   b fish on the shelf?
3 Is there an   c oranges in the basket?
4 There is a   d six pies on the desk.
5 There are   e glass of milk on the table.

23 Ask and answer about your toys.

 Is there a doll on your bed?
Yes, there is.
Are there blocks in your toy box?
No, there aren't.

Culture Connection | Around the World

24 How many toys do you have? What's your favorite?

I have a lot of toys. My favorite is my plane. It's gray.

25 Listen, read, and point. How many toys does Emma have?

My Toy Box

This is my toy box. There are toys in it.

1 I like my airplane and my train. The airplane is red, blue, and white. It's from the U.K. The train is wooden. It's from China.

2 My favorite toys are my dolls. They're from Russia. There is a big doll, and there are small dolls in it. The small dolls go into the big doll. The last doll is a baby. The dolls are colorful. I love my Russian dolls. I play with them every day.

26 Circle **T** for true and **F** for false.

1 The airplane is from China. T F
2 The Russian dolls are from Japan. T F
3 There are small dolls in the big Russian doll. T F
4 The small dolls go in the big doll. T F
5 Emma has a train from the U.K. T F

27 **Look at 25. Read and circle.**

1 This is my **small / toy** box.
2 The airplane is red, blue, and **white / gray**.
3 The train is **Russian / wooden**.
4 The last doll is a **baby / toy**.
5 Emma has one **big / small** doll.
6 The airplane is from **China / the U.K.**

28 **Draw Russian dolls for you. Talk with a partner.**

What color are your dolls?

They're green and yellow.

How many small dolls are ir the big doll?

Six.

THINK BIG Does your country have a special toy? What is it?

culture connection (favorite toys) Unit 8

Values | **Share your toys.**

 29 **Listen and find the picture. Then listen and repeat.**

1

2

3

4

30 Look and number. Then say.

a

b

c

Sharing is fun!

Here's my car. Let's share.

Okay. Thank you!

THINK BIG Is it good to share your toys? Why?

146 Unit 8 values

qu, x, y | **Phonics**

225
 31 Listen, look, and repeat.

1 qu   x   3 y

226
 32 Listen and find. Then say.

yell   quick   six

227
 33 Listen and blend the sounds.

1 qu-a-ck   quack   2 b-o-x   box   3 y-e-s   yes
4 o-x   ox   5 f-o-x   fox   6 y-u-m   yum

228
34 Underline **qu**, **x**, and **y**. Then listen and chant.

Six quick foxes,
In a yellow box!

Review

 35 **Listen and circle. Then say.**

36 **Look at 35. Ask and answer.**

Where are the action figures?

Where are the planes?

They're on the bed and under the chair.

They're on the shelf and under the desk.

Review

37 **Look and match.**

1 blocks   a

2 bike   b

3 cars   c

4 game   d

5 puppet   e

6 train   f

38 **Read and match.**

1 There's   a in the backpack.
2 There are ten   b two shoes under the desk.
3 There are   c salad on the table?
4 There's an   d a puppet on the bed.
5 There aren't pens   e egg in the box.
6 Is there a   f balls on the shelf.

I Can
- [ ] name toys.
- [ ] say where something is.
- [ ] talk about sharing my toys.

Play Time

1 Listen, look, and say.

1 catching
2 throwing
3 hitting
4 kicking
5 dancing
6 singing
7 skating
8 riding
9 jumping rope

2 Listen, find, and say.   3 Play a game.

4 Listen and sing. Then look at 1 and find.

Play Time Is Cool!

We like play time at our school.
Singing and dancing,
Throwing and catching.
Play time is cool at our school!

I'm throwing the ball.
It's so much fun!
Are you
Hitting and running?
Yes, and it's fun.

We're kicking the ball
And trying to score.
It's so much fun.
Let's play some more.

Chorus

5 Listen and ✓.

1 a    b    2 a    b

6 Look at **5**. Ask and answer.

 Are you kicking?

Yes, I am.

THINK BIG Look at **1**. What are they doing with their feet? What are they doing with their hands?

Story

7 Listen and read. What's Ann doing?

8 Look at the story. Number the pictures in order.

a

b

c

d

THINK BIG Imagine you are getting ready for bed. Act it out and say what you are doing!

Language in Action

9 Listen. Help Tim and Jane make sentences.

- jumping rope
- throwing
- skating
- riding

Is she | singing | ?
Yes, she is | .
Are they | dancing | ?
No, they aren't | .

10 Listen and number.

a. 
b. 
c. 
d. 
e. 
f.

154 Unit 9 language practice (*Are you dancing? Yes, I am.*)

Language in Action

11 Listen and stick. Then say.

12 Look at 11. Ask and answer.

Is she running?

No, she isn't. She's jumping rope.

13 Draw and say. Are you throwing a ball?

Content Connection | Physical Education

 14 **Listen, repeat, and find. Then ask and answer.**

> What games do you play in the playground?

> Hopscotch and jumping rope.

 15 **Listen, read, and point. What's her favorite game?**

climbing

jumping rope

hide and seek

hopscotch

tag

1. Playing games with my friends is a lot of fun. We play in the school playground.
2. We climb to the top of the bars. Up! Up! Up! We also jump rope. My friends jump very fast. Jump! Jump! Jump!
3. We play hide and seek, too. I count to ten, then I look for my friends. 1, 2, 3…Where are you?
4. We also play hopscotch. Hop! Hop! Hop!
5. My favorite game of all is tag. Let's run! Run! Run! Tag, you're it!

 **THINK BIG** Who do you play with? What are your favorite games?

16 Read and number. Then listen and check.

a Let's play tag! ☐ b Let's jump rope! ☐ c Let's play hopscotch! ☐

d Let's play hide and seek! ☐ e Let's climb! ☐

17 Look at 15. Match. Then act and say.

1 1, 2, 3… Where are you?   a hopscotch
2 Hop, hop, hop!   b hide and seek
3 Let's run! Run! Run!   c jumping rope
4 Jump! Jump! Jump!   d climbing
5 Up! Up! Up!   e tag

Jump! Jump! Jump!

PROJECT

18 Make a Play Time poster. Then present it to the class.

Playtime is fun. I play tag, and I jump rope. My favorite game is hopscotch.

content connection (playground games) Unit 9 **157**

Grammar

19 Look, listen, and point. Then say.

1 I like dancing, but I don't like jumping rope. I like dancing with my friends. I like fruit, but I don't like salad. My favorite fruit is apples. I also like animals. My favorite animal is a horse.

2 I don't like hopscotch, but I like playing tag. I don't like salad, but I like pasta. I also don't like frogs, but I like snakes and hamsters.

like…	don't like…
I like dancing.	I don't like hopscotch.
I like fruit.	I don't like salad.
I like horses.	I don't like frogs.
He/She/It likes…	He/She/It doesn't like…

> I like dancing. I don't like jumping rope.

158 Unit 9

Grammar

20 **Look and write like/don't like.**

1 I _____ kittens.
2 I _____ snakes.
3 I _____ spiders.
4 I _____ turtles.
5 I _____ puppies.
6 I _____ horses.

| kittens ✗ |
| snakes ✓ |
| spiders ✓ |
| turtles ✓ |
| puppies ✗ |
| horses ✗ |

21 **Read and circle.**

1 I **likes** / **like** board games.
2 Sally **likes** / **like** CDs.
3 Ben **doesn't like** / **don't like** dancing.
4 I **don't like** / **doesn't like** playing tag.
5 Paul **like** / **likes** computers.
6 Patty **don't like** / **doesn't like** watching TV.

22 **Draw three things you like and three things you don't like. Talk with a partner.**

I like playing hopscotch.
I don't like jumping rope.

grammar (*I like dancing. He doesn't like salad.*) Unit 9

Culture Connection | Around the World

23 Look and listen. Say and do the action.

Rock, Paper, Scissors
Same Game... Different Name!

24 Listen and read. Where do they call this game Cachipún?

1 Canada

I'm Eva. I'm nine. I play Rock, Paper, Scissors in Canada. I play with my sisters and my best friend, Tina. I always win.

2 Japan

I'm Michio. I'm seven. I'm from Japan. I play this game at school with my friends. We call it Janken. I sometimes win.

3 Chile

I'm Raúl. I'm eight. I'm from Chile. We play this game, too. We call it Cachipún. My brother, Martin, is the best player in our family.

25 **Look at 24. Read and ✓.**

1 Who always wins?   Tina ☐   Eva ☐
2 Who plays with his friends?   Martin ☐ Michio ☐
3 Who plays with his brother?   Michio ☐ Raúl ☐
4 Who sometimes wins?   Michio ☐ Eva ☐
5 Who is the best player?   Tina ☐   Martin ☐
6 Who plays with her sisters?   Eva ☐   Tina ☐

26 **Look, listen, and say. Play with a friend.**

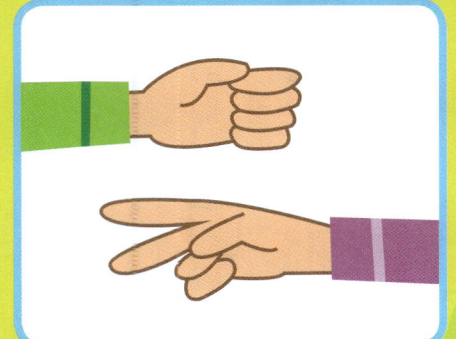

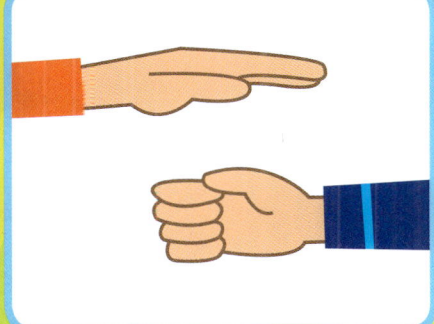

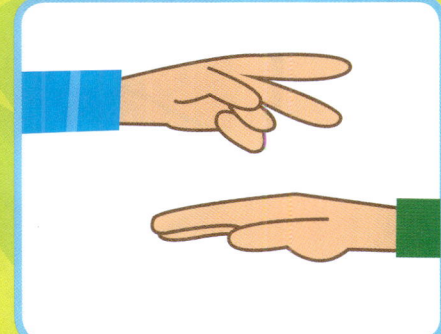

1 Rock breaks scissors. Rock wins!
2 Paper covers rock. Paper wins!
3 Scissors cut paper. Scissors win!

THINK BIG Do you play Rock, Paper, Scissors in your country? What do you call it? Who do you play with? Who wins?

Values | Take care of your body.

27 Listen and find the picture. Then listen and repeat.

1    2    3

28 Listen and number. Then say.

a

Get enough exercise.

b

Get enough sleep.

c

Get enough food and drink.

THINK BIG How do you take care of your body?

ss, z, zz | Phonics

29 **Listen, look, and repeat.**

1 **ss** 2 **z** 3 **zz**

30 **Listen and find. Then say.**

  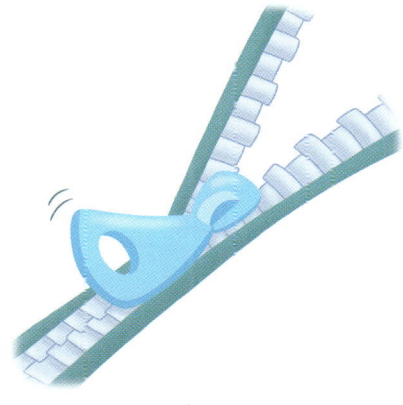

bu**zz** ki**ss** **z**ip

31 **Listen and blend the sounds.**

1 m-e-ss mess   2 z-a-p zap   3 f-i-zz fizz
4 m-i-ss miss   5 j-a-zz jazz

32 **Underline ss, z, and zz. Then listen and chant.**

Buzz goes the bee.
Zip, zap!
It misses me!

Review

 **259**

33 Listen and circle.

34 Look at 33. Ask and answer.

 Is he jumping rope?

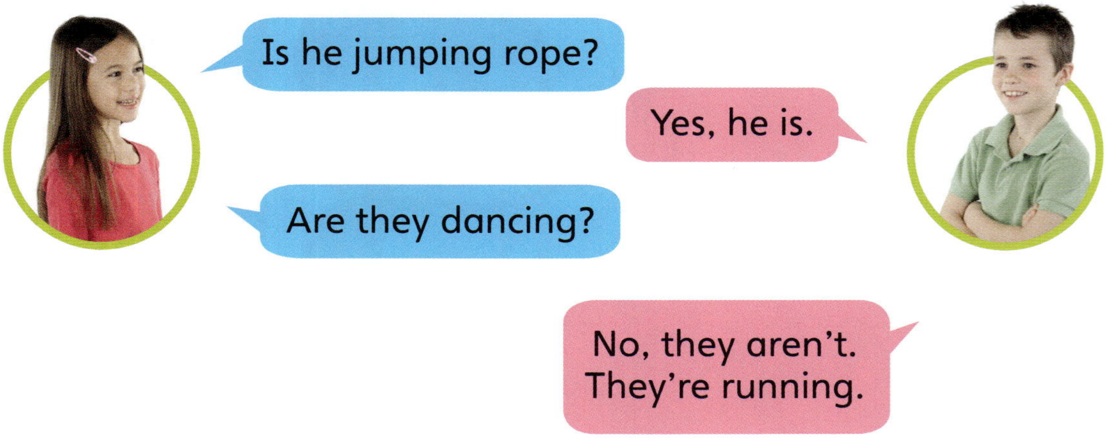

Yes, he is.

Are they dancing?

No, they aren't. They're running.

164 Unit 9 review

Review

35 Listen and number.

a
b
c
d
e
f

36 Read and match.

a

b

I like
I don't like

c

d

I Can
- ☐ talk about actions and what I like/don't like.
- ☐ talk about games children play.
- ☐ say how I take care of my body.

Checkpoint | Units 7–9

Do I Know It?

1 Look and circle. Practice.

😊 I know this.   😕 I don't know this.

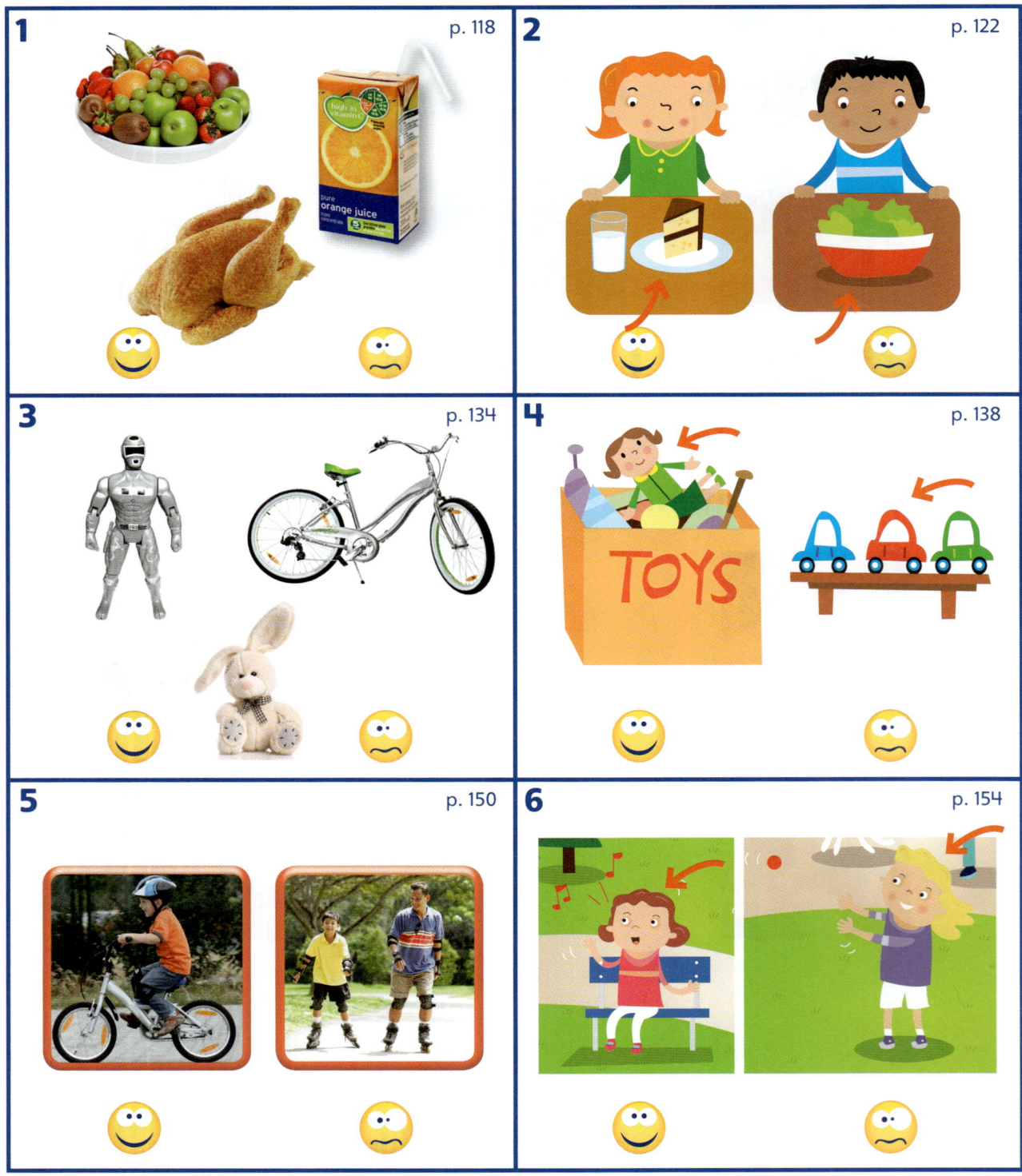

I Can Do It!

 Get ready.

A Look. Listen to the questions. Circle the correct words.

1 It's on the **shelf** / **table**.
2 They're **on** / **under** the bed.
3 Yes, **he** / **she** does.

B Listen again and check. Then practice with a partner.

C Look at **A**. Answer these questions with a partner.
  1 What food can you see? What drinks can you see?
  2 How many toys can you see? What are they?
  3 What day is it?

Checkpoint Units 7–9 **167**

Checkpoint | Units 7-9

3 Draw.

STEP 1 Cut out the outline on page 185.

STEP 2 Fold the paper to make a book.

STEP 3 Write in your book. Color the front.
Now you're ready to **Go!**

4 Go!

A Read your book with three classmates. Take turns. Write the presents.

Classmate	Present
Bruno	a train
1	
2	
3	

B Look at your books. Answer these questions with a partner.
1 Page 2: What are they doing?
2 Page 3: What food and drink do they have?
3 Page 3: Where's the cat?
4 Page 4: How many presents can you see?

5 Draw.

All About Me

My favorite food is:

My favorite toy is:

Do I Know It Now?

6 Think about it.

A Go to page **166**. Look and circle again.

B Check (✔).
- ☐ I can ask my teacher for help.
- ☐ I can practice.

7 Rate this Checkpoint. Color the stars.

easy   hard

fun   not fun

Units 7–9 Exam Preparation

– Part A –

Listen and draw lines. There is one example.

– Part B –

Look and read. Write *yes* or *no*.

Examples

The boy has ice cream.	yes
The ducks are swimming in the ocean.	no

Questions

1 A girl is riding a red bike. _____

2 The grandma is reading a book. _____

3 A girl is catching a ball. _____

4 A man is drinking milk. _____

5 A woman is eating chips. _____

Young Learners English Practice Starters: Listening A

– 5 questions –

 Look at the picture. Now listen and color. There is one example.

172 Listening A

Young Learners English Practice Starters: Listening B

– 5 questions –

 Look at the pictures. Now listen and draw lines. There is one example.

Listening B 173

Young Learners English Practice Starters: Listening C

– 5 questions –

 Look at the pictures. Now listen and check (✓). There is one example.

What's she wearing?

A ✓   B ☐   C ☐

1 Is your brother eating?

A ☐   B ☐   C ☐

2 What's she doing?

A ☐   B ☐   C ☐

3 What are they?

A ☐

B ☐

C ☐

4 What are the cats doing?

A ☐

B ☐

C ☐

5 What are his favorite clothes?

A ☐

B ☐

C ☐

Young Learners English Practice Starters: Reading & Writing A

– 5 questions –

Look and check. Put a check (✔) or an (✘) in the box.
There are two examples.

Examples

This is a chair.

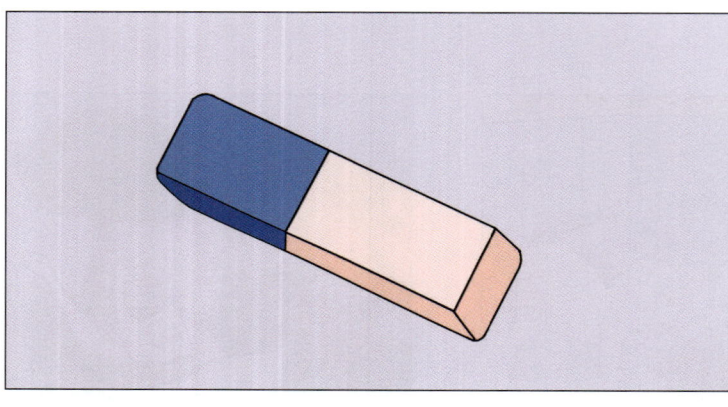

This is a ruler.

Questions

1

This is a baby. ☐

2

This is a foot. ☐

3

This is a book. ☐

4

This is a sister. ☐

5

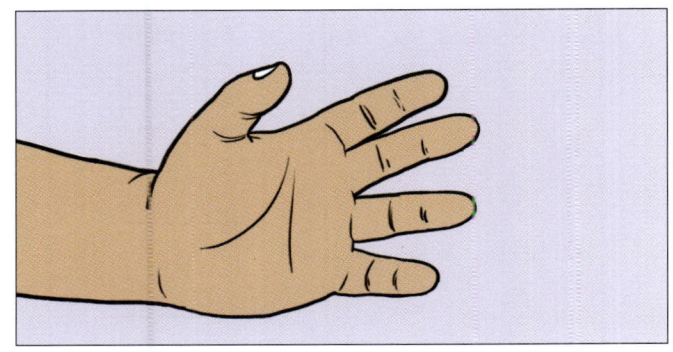

This is a hand. ☐

Young Learners English Practice Starters: Reading & Writing B

– 5 questions –

Look and read. Write *yes* or *no*.

Examples

The farmer is wearing boots.	yes
The dog is running.	no

Questions

1. The girl is feeding the ducks. _____

2. The chickens are eating. _____

3. The girl has short hair. _____

4. The boy is reading a book. _____

5. The farmer has a red shirt. _____

Young Learners English Practice Starters: Reading & Writing C

– 5 questions –

Look at the pictures. Look at the letters. Write the words.

Example

t r a i n   a r n t i

Questions

1

_ _ _ _ _ _   g n a o e r

2

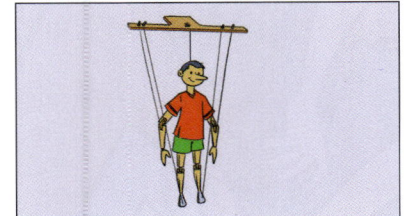

_ _ _ _ _ _   t p u p e p

3

_ _ _ _ _   l a d s a

4

_ _ _ _ _ _   t a k s e s

5

_ _ _ _ _ _ _ _   d i n s h c a w

Young Learners English Practice Starters: Speaking

 # Cutouts for Page 60, Checkpoint Units 1–3

Checkpoint Cutouts Units 1–3

Cutouts for Page 114, Checkpoint Units 4–6

Checkpoint Cutouts Units 4–6 183

Cutouts for Page 168, Checkpoint Units 7–9

It's My Party!

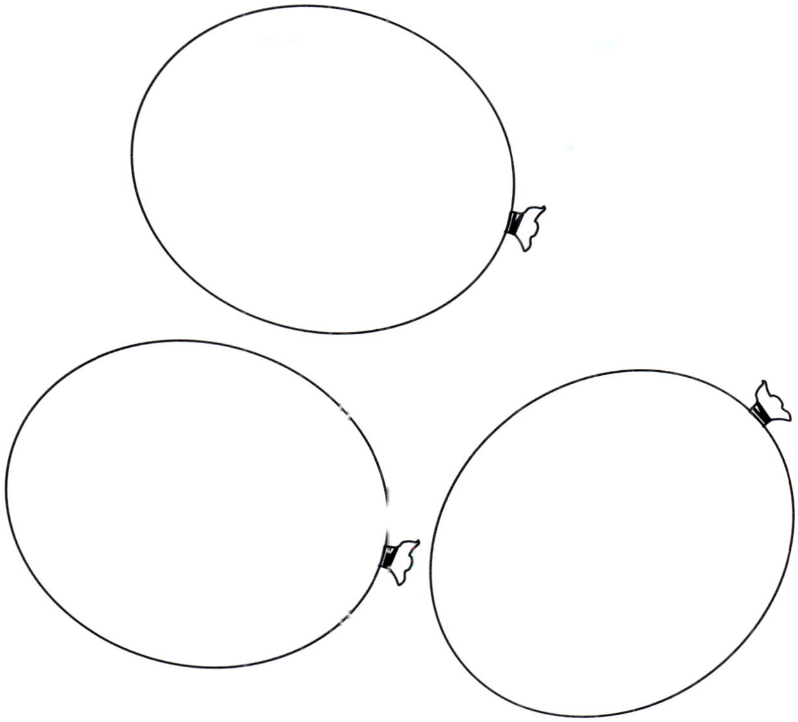

_____
[name]

I have a present. It's a
_____ . I'm happy today!
[toy]

4

Cutouts for Page 168, Checkpoint Units 7–9

Today is _____ .
[day]

2

My friends are eating _____ .
[food]

3

186 Checkpoint Cutouts Units 7–9

Big English Song

From the mountaintops to the bottom of the sea,
From a big blue whale to a baby bumblebee —
If you're big, if you're small, you can have it all,
And you can be anything you want to be!

It's bigger than you. It's bigger than me.
There's so much to do, and there's so much to see!
The world is big and beautiful, and so are we!
Think big! Dream big! Big English!

So in every land, from the desert to the sea,
We can all join hands and be one big family.
If we love, if we care, we can go anywhere!
The world belongs to everyone; it's ours to share.

It's bigger than you. It's bigger than me.
There's so much to do, and there's so much to see!
The world is big and beautiful, and so are we!
Think big! Dream big! Big English!

It's bigger than you. It's bigger than me.
There's so much to do, and there's so much to see!
The world is big and beautiful and waiting for me.
A one, two, three...
Think big! Dream big! Big English!

Pearson Education Limited
Edinburgh Gate
Harlow
Essex CM20 2JE
England
and Associated Companies throughout the world.
www.pearsonelt.com/bigenglish

© Pearson Education Limited 2015

Authorised adaptation from the United States edition entitled Big English, 1st Edition, by Mario Herrera and Christopher Sol Cruz. Published by Pearson Education Inc. © 2013 by Pearson Education, Inc.

The right of Mario Herrera and Christopher Sol Cruz to be identified as the authors of this Work have been asserted by them in accordance with the Copyright, Designs and Patents Act 1988.

All rights reserved; no part of this publication may be reproduced, stored in a retrieval system, or transmitted in any form or by any means, electronic, mechanical, photocopying, recording, or otherwise without the prior written permission of the Publishers.

First published 2015
Eighth impression 2019
ISBN: 978-1-4479-8924-0
Set in Heinemann Roman
Printed in Italy by L.E.G.O. S.p.A.

Acknowledgements
The publisher would like to thank the following for their kind permission to reproduce photographs:

(Key: b-bottom; c-centre; l-left; r-right; t-top)

123RF.com: 123RF Limited 160 (Japan), Alexey Astakhov 142 (pizza), andersonrise 128 (Russia), 129/4, Cathy Yeulet 106/25 (Elina), cypher0x 144bl, Darrin Henry 18/19 (4), 25 (d), Dylan Burrill 52 (a), gorgev 106/25 (I), Holger Schmidt 142 (check tablecloth), Hongqi Zhang 106/25 (Sharon), Ivonne Wierink 144br, ka2shka 143/21 (TCL), Karin Lau 90b, Martin Galabov 52 (b), 52 (c), 52 (d), Nat Sukukawadee 106/25 (3), nerthuz 143/21 (TR), Nicolas Nadjar 106/25 (2), pogonici 143/21 (TL), Polsin Janpangpen 106/24 (rabbit), szefei 128 (Korea), 129/3, Tracy Whiteside 106/25 (Zack); **Age Fotostock Spain S.L.:** Ruth Black 104 (d), 108 (playing), Robert Daly 154 (f), Hybrid Images / Cultura 108 (brushing), Image Source 119/5 (4), Insy Shah / Gulf Images 16/15 (3), DU BOISBERRANGER Jean 76 (a), Juice Images 162/27 (2); **Alamy Images:** Aflo Foto Agency 151/1 (a), Anna Maloverjan / Alamy 70/15 (centre right), Caro / Alamy 92/1, Chris Ryan / Alamy 86/15 (4 right), dave stamboulis / Alamy 86/15 (1 left), Friedrich Stark 20/1, imageBROKER 165/36 (d girl)), IMAGEMORE Co., Ltd. / Alamy 70/15 (centre left), Jeff Morgan 09 156 (skipping), JTB MEDIA CREATION, Inc. 76 (b), Jurgen Magg 156 (hide & seek), Kuttig - People - 2 156 (tag), Semen Lihodeev 64/2, Marco Secchi 74bc, Michael Matthews 86/14 (3), MBI / Alamy 42l, 58/6 (left), 130/28 (b), Michael Willis / Alamy 48 (computer), Neil Tingle 74bl, nikreates 118/4, 133/2 (a), 142 (orange juice), 162/28 (c right), 166/1 (TR), ONOKY - Photononstop / Alamy 27t, 32, 58/3, Richard Heyes 143/21 (TCR), RubberBall 20/3, Sally and Richard Greenhill 156 (hopscotch), 158/2 (T), sayoga / Alamy 140/15 (d), Septemberlegs / Alamy 86/15 (2 right), StockImages / Alamy 124/15 (sweet - sugar), Tetra Images / Alamy 41/4 (b), 92/4, 126/2, Wildscape 156 (climbing); **Corbis:** Andersen Ross / Blend Images 54 (a), Heide Benser 80/7, Hero Images 92/2, 126/4, JGI / Jamie Grill, Ocean 26, 30, 35, Vast Photography / First Light / Corbis 54 (b), Wavebreak Media Ltd ; **DK Images:** Andy Crawford 9/17 (point), 18/20 (2), 51 (feet); **Fotolia.com:** air 54 (c), Alexandr Ozerov 70/14 (l), amidala 106/24 (horse), 111/36 (d), Andres Rodriguez 110br, apops 33bl, 33bc, 34/1, 34/3, 79r, Arsgera 89/3, 134/8, Atiketta Sangasaeng 10/1, bARTiko 140/15 (a), byrdyak 88 (d), 96/6, 112/5 (L), 158/1 (B), CandyBox Images 38br, Chris leachman 124/14 (3), dave timms 140/15 (b), Delmas Lehman 111/36 (a), dimedrol68 10/7, 58/2 (pencil), emirkoo 106/24 (dog), 111/36 (c), 126/5, Eric Isselée 57/1 (b), Ever 124/15 (salty - crisps), 125/17 (crisps), fir4ik 48/2, ftfoxfoto 102/14 (4), Gabees 89/1, 95/3, 134/3, 146/4, gemenacom 64/10, 71 (t-shirt), gena96 124/14 (6), 124/15 (salty - chips), 125/17 (fries), Giuseppe Porzani 118/11, 125/17 (pasta), 133/1 (b), Giuseppe_R 41/1 (b), 72/2, 73/3, hellkitty 140/15 (c), heros1973 118/1, 125/17 (cake), 128/23 (L), iofoto 18/19 (5), 151/2 (a), itsallgood 57/4 (a), Iuliia Metkalova 16/15 (2), ivan gusev 140tl, Ivonne Wierink 10/10, jackmicro 86/15 (2 left), 86/15 (4 left), jjpixs 74tc, 150/3, 151tl, 165/35 (b), JM Fotografie, jo 70/14 (2), Joanna Zielinska 150/8, 154 (a), 165/35 (e), 166/5 (L), kilukilu 64/11, 71 (socks), Kimsonal 102/15 (chicken), Konovalov Pavel 64/4, 71 (hat), 112/1 (hat), Kzenon 80/10, 84/1 (b), 95 (a), laszlolorik 16/14 (3), leonidp 96/7, 111/37 (b), 112/5 (C), magann 70/14 (3), Marco Uliana, Maria Mitrofanova 64/7, mdorottya 48 (b), Michael Ireland 150/2, mm3104 57/4 (b), Monkey Business 124/15 (sweet - cookies), 125/17 (cookies), natavin 134/7, 166/3 (B), Natika 124/14 (5), nbiebach 96/1, 106/24 (cat), Nenov Brothers 89/4, 134/5, 135 (a), 149 (f), nerthuz 90c, Noam 41/1 (a), 72/1, 79l, Pavel Losevsky 48/1, PhG 86/15 (1 right), picsfive 48 (ice cream), 124/14 (2), 125/17 (chocolate), Picture-Factory 57/2 (a), pio3 150/6, 151/2 (b), RainLedy 48 (perfume), rakjung2 96/5, 111/37 (d), Roijoy 71bl, RTimages 118/2, 125/17 (fruit), 133/4 (c), 158/1 (T), 166/1 (TL), Rudolf Tepfenhart 70/14 (6), Schlierner 10/6, Sergii Figurnyi 86/15 (3 left), SergiyN 34/4, 41/3 (b), 73/2, simmittorok 10/9, sommersby 64/12, 112/1 (shirt), stockphoto-graf 133/4 (b), sumnersgraphicsinc 124/15 (sweet - chocolate), tan4ikk 130/28 (c), Tatyana Gladskih 16/14 (2), 18/19 (3), Tetiana Zbrodko 95/1, 134/10, 146/1, 149 (d), thawats 51 (hands), The Josh 70/14 (4), thepoo 16/14 (4), Vaida 102/15 (cow), 104 (c), Vasiliy Koval 46b, 57/1 (a), vgm6 102/15 (dog), Viktor 118/9, 118/10, 124/14 (4), 124/15 (salty - salt), 125/17 (chicken), 125/17 (salt), 130/29 (a), 133/1 (c), 133/3 (c), 166/1 (B), Vit 134/1, 166/3 (TL), vlorzor 64/13, 71 (shorts), windu 64/6, 71 (trousers), Wojciech Sobiech 41/3 (a), xalanx 104 (a), 108 (feeding), Yasonya 118/6, 132/2 (c), 133/4 (a), Ziablik 134/11, 149 (c); **Getty Images:** Andrew Bain 70/15 (centre), Anwar Hussein / WireImage 74br, Beto Hacker / The Image Bank 80/5, 84/4 (b), Jon Shireman / The Image Bank 86/14 (l), Paul Bradbury 80/4, 112/3 (TR), Andrea Chu 162/27 (l), Peter Dazeley 81, 84/1 (a), Digital Vision 119/6 (2), 25 (a), 80/12, 84/3 (b), Fuse 80/11, 95 (c), 103 (R), Peter Cade / Iconica 80/1, 112/3 (TL), Bruno Morandi / Robert Harding World Imagery 86/14 (2), Susanna Price / Dk Images 80/3, 95 (b), Kraig Scarbinsky / Digital Vision 92/3, Photolibrary / David Page Photography 165/36 (a), Ryan McVay / Stone 84/2 (b), Sophia Vourdoukis / Stone 80/8, 84/3 (a), 112/4 (L), Vstock LLC 95 (d); **Glow Images:** Alex Mares-Manton 154 (b), 165/35 (f), 166/5 (R); **Imagestate Media:** Phovoir 9/18 (b); **Pearson Education:** 5, 43, 46tl, 47t, 49bl, 50 (desk & eraser), 87br, 96/8, 103 (poster), 125bl (poster), 158/2 (B); **Pearson Education Ltd:** Studio 8 89/2, 95/2, 134/6, 149 (b), Trevor Clifford 6tl, 6tr, 6bl, 6br, 7l, 7r, 8l, 8r, 9/17 (clap), 11l, 11r, 15l, 15r, 18/20 (1), 19 (boy), 19 (girl), 21, 27bl, 27br, 31l, 31r, 33tl, 33tr, 47bl, 47br, 49t, 51bl, 51br, 53l, 53r, 56bl, 56br, 65cl, 65cr, 71cr, 74 (girl), 75l, 75r, 76bl, 76br, 85l, 85r, 87tl, 87tr, 89bl, 89br, 91l, 91r, 97bl, 97br, 101l, 101r, 103tl, 103tr, 105l, 105r, 107, 108bl, 108br, 119bl, 119br, 123l, 123r, 125/18 (right), 127l, 127r, 132l, 132r, 135bl, 135br, 139l, 139r, 140tr, 141tl, 141tr, 143bl, 143br, 144cl, 145l, 145r, 148l, 148r, 151bl, 151br, 155l, 155r, 158/1 (girl), 158/2 (boy), 164l, 164r, Rafal Trubisz 144/24 (TL); **Pearson Education Ltd:** Trevor Clifford 9/17 (stand), 9/18 (a), 9/18 (c), 9/18 (d), 18/20 (3), 18/20 (4); **PhotoDisc:** Tony Gable. C Squared Studios 48 (c); **Photolibrary:** Image Source 150/5, 158/1 (C); **Shutterstock.com:** 142 (sandwich), 162/28 (c left), AnetaPics 110/2, Anneka 102/14 (2), 104 (f), 111/37 (a), Yuri Arcurs 18/19 (1), 25 (c), 42r, 58/5, Arvind Balaraman 119tl, Gyorgy Barna 80/2, 84/2 (a), 162/27 (3), Chris Bence 118/7, 128/23 (R), 133/3 (a), Ingvar Bjork 10/5, 58/2 (pen), Ruth Black, Mihai Blanaru 74tl, 165/35 (a), BlankaB 106/25 (Flag - Australia), Bragin Alexey 124/14 (1), 125/17 (sugar), Brooke Becker 16/14 (1), charnsitr 106/25 (Flag - USA), chatursunil 57/2 (b), Palle Christensen 125/17 (orange juice), Chros 160/1-3, Condor 36 128 (United States), 129/2, David Pirvu 41/2 (b), 72/3, DenisNata 119/5 (3), Digital Media Pro 48/4, discpicture 40, djgis 96/10, 111/36 (b), Doug Lemke 86/15 (3 right), Jaimie Duplass 150/9, 157f, ffolas 133/1 (a), 142 (salad), Mike Flippo 162/28 (a), Fotogroove 106/25 (Flag - Japan), Gelpi JM 49c, Gemenacom 9/19 (left), 9/19 (right), gengirl 102/15 (cat), Volodymyr Goinyk 70/14 (5), Golden Pixels LLC 108 (walking), Greenland 150/7, 151/1 (b), Happy person 48 (a), 65b, Margo Harrison 134/2, 135 (c), 146/3, haveseen 80/6, 112/3 (B), 126/3, Darrin Henry 17, 41/2 (a), 73/1, Horiyan 118/5, 130/29 (b), Mau Horng 124/15 (sweet - cake), 133/3 (b), iofoto 106/25 (Reiko), Eric Isselee 95/4, 97tl (goat), 97tr (goat), 110/4, Jacek Chabraszewski 165/36 (c), Jenkedco 128 (Mexico), 129/1, Karkas 64/5, 64/8, Katstudio 124/15 (salty - pizza), Joana Kruse 119/5 (1), Lucie Lang 10/3, 50 (crayon), 58/1 (crayon), Aliaksei Lasevich 70/15 (bottom), 74tr, Lenkadan 97 (a), 110/1, Leroy Harvey 142 (burger), Alexander Mak 88 (a), 102/14 (3), mamahoohooba 141b, Martin Nemec 88 (c), 96/3, 97 (b), 112/5 (R), mathom 88 (b), 102/14 (1), Vladimir Melnikov 154 (e), michaeljung 18/19 (2), 25 (b), 41b (c), 65tr, Stuart Monk 86/14 (4), Monkey Business Images 34/2, 41b (a), 58/4, 103br, 119/5 (2), Pavel V Mukhin 64/1, 71 (boots), 112/1 (boots), Amy Myers 150/4, 165/35 (d), Lisovskaya Natalia 10/2, Nattika 165/35 (d cheese)), Nenov Brothers Images 144/24 (TCL), Nikonboy 90tr, Michal Ninger 97 (c), 110/3, nito 144/24 (TCR), nrt 118/8, 130/29 (d), 158/2 (C), Olga Syzranova 80/9, 84/4 (a), 95 (e), 126/1, 162/28 (b), Alon Othnay 154 (c), M. Unal Ozmen 125/17 (ice cream), panco971 165/36 (b), PhotoNAN 64/9, Olga Popova, ppfoto13 64/3, Alexander Raths 46tr, 58/6 (right), 119tr, Randy Rimland 96/4, Karen Roach 10/8, 118/3, 128/23 (C), 133/2 (b), Rob Marmion 20/2, Anatoliy Samara 16/15 (1), 157b, Sean Locke Photography 160 (Chile), Anna Sedneva 95/4, 97t (oats), 110/4 (oats), SergiyN 69r, 112/2 (R), Valery Shklovskiy 96/2, Roman Sigaev, Sofarina79 154 (d), Stephanie Frey 144cr, Margaret M Stewart 10/4, Kuttelvaserova Stuchelova 33br, swissmacky 57/3 (b), Tatik22 134/9, 149 (a), Tony Taylor 111/37 (c), Leah-Anne Thompson 150/1, 165/35 (c), juan carlos tinjaca 49br, V_Krv 48 (MP3), V. J. Matthew 91/2, Val Thoermer 130/28 (a), Valentina_S 96/9, viki2win 160 (Canada), VojtechVlk 41/4 (a), Tatyana Vychegzhanina 151tr, wacpan 134/1, 135 (b), 144/24 (TR), 146/2, 149 (e), 166/3 (TR), YanLev 41b (b), 73/4, Kisialiou Yury 48 (d), ZouZou 165/36 (d boy));

Stickers

Unit 1, page 15

Unit 2, page 31

Unit 3, page 47

Stickers

Unit 4, page 69

Unit 5, page 85

Unit 6, page 101

Stickers

Unit 7, page 123

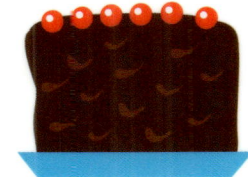

Unit 8, page 139

Unit 9, page 155